JESSIE PENN-LEWIS

A LIFE MOLDED BY THE CROSS

JESSIE PENN-LEWIS

A LIFE MOLDED BY THE CROSS

WRITTEN BY

J.C. METCALFE

CLC PUBLICATIONS
Fort Washington, PA 19034

Jessie Penn-Lewis: A Life Molded by the Cross
Published by CLC Publications

U.S.A.
P.O. Box 1449, Fort Washington, PA 19034

UNITED KINGDOM
CLC International (UK)
Unit 5, Glendale Avenue, Sandycroft, Flintshire, CH5 2QP

Previously published under the title *Molded by the Cross*

First published by the Overcomer Press in England
Original title: *In the Mould of the Cross*
Re-edited by Robert Delancy

This printing 2019

Printed in the United States of America

ISBN (paperback): 978-1-61958-304-7

CONTENTS

FOREWORD

Soon after the home call of Jessie Penn-Lewis, her successor as editor of *The Overcomer*, Mary Garrard, settled down to write her biography. It was a labor of love. A mass of material was care fully collected, and then, after much thought and prayer, selection was made. So it was that a book *Mrs. Penn-Lewis—A Memoir* was published in 1930, a second edition being printed in 1947. It has now been out of print for several years; and the natural reaction to the issue of another edition is: "But who will be interested?"

The fact is, however, that over the last few years the demand for books and book lets written by Jessie Penn-Lewis has been steadily rising; and lately we have had a spate of inquiries as to whether there is any biography of her in existence. For this reason it seemed that we ought to consider a reprint. But this is not going to be a reprint! And I shall have to go rather a long way around to explain the reason!

Mrs. Penn-Lewis was granted by God a special enduement of power for service, which has meant not only that her spoken ministry was greatly effective but also that today, years later, her messages in print are still fresh and vital, and are being used to bring help and blessing to many all over the world. It is recorded that on one occasion a gentleman with a strong prejudice against the ministry of women heard her speak at a conference, and said to her afterwards: "I would not have believed it possible, had I not seen it, that God would use a *woman* like that." "God never does use a woman like that," was her quick response, "or a *man* either! God only uses the *new creation*."

This, in a day when in Christian work men are set on pedestals and their natural gifts made much of, is a healthy reminder that God does not see things as we do but works in our world by His Spirit using the weak, the foolish and the base things to fulfill His purpose. His way of fruitfulness is that of life out of death. Dr. P.T. Forsyth emphasizes this for us when he says: "Christ dies like a corn of wheat sinking into the ground to rot, but His harvest grows all over the world. So our fruitless efforts for souls will germinate yonder, as mummy wheat is said to sprout in soil today." In Mrs. Penn-Lewis' own words: "From the hour the Spirit of God whispered 'Crucified' to me, I also saw clearly the principle of *death with Christ as the basis for the full working of God through the believer*."

It is the broad principles of God's ways with men that we need so carefully to apply to our lives, not the details of someone else's experience; and a law we glimpse behind God's dealings with Jessie Penn-Lewis is that, whatever the phraseology we employ, the fullness of the Holy Spirit does not minister to our own enjoyment or simply for the building up of our own lives but for the *fulfillment of God's purposes* of love and grace for others. "The manifestation of the Spirit is given to every man to profit withal." The Holy Spirit in all His splendid power led the Victor to Calvary. The profit that has accrued to men from the cross is boundless. What a stream of blessing, for instance, still flows today by way of the pen of the lonely prisoner in Rome, the apostle Paul, who once wrote: "So then death worketh in us, but life in you" (2 Cor. 4:12).

In compiling this book, then, the main aim has been to give as simply and briefly as possible a picture of the way that God dealt with and poured life through His servant-life which still flows today. As far as possible, her own words will be used. This would have been a most arduous if not impossible task without Mary Garrard's collection and handling of the valuable material at her disposal, and I can only express my very great indebtedness to my late friend and predecessor as present editor of *The Overcomer.*

On the title page of the original memoir there appears the Old Syriac version of John 7:38–39, which reads: "He that believeth into Me, out of the depths of his life shall pour torrents of living water. This spake He of the Spirit." This is what God has done through Jessie Penn-Lewis, and longs to do for you and me. There can be no shadow of doubt as to His willingness and ability to accomplish this in us if we too are content to tread the path which leads continually through death into life.

CHAPTER ONE

BACKGROUNDS AND BEGINNINGS

THE scene is a large convention tent. The congregation is mainly composed of Christian leaders and ministers of many denominations, representative of the finest elements in the spiritual life of Scotland. The platform has always been reserved for men, and outstanding men at that. Today tradition has been set aside, and speaking in a hush indicative of rapt attention is a small, frail-looking woman. Her message is centered in the cross of Christ. It is a rare thing to hear "the message of the cross" preached in any other aspect than its relationship to the forgiveness of sins and our acceptance before God. Sometimes it *is* shown to be the one place of victory over the power of sin, in accordance with the teaching of Romans 6. But here was something that led yet further into God's ways with His children. There is a place where the nature and outlook of the Lord Jesus begin to over shadow a life that is yielded to Him. To use Jessie Penn-Lewis' own words:

> On the Godward side the soul will be led from faith to faith, from strength to strength, from glory to glory; while on the earth ward side, the outward man is 'always delivered to death' and becomes increasingly a partaker of the afflictions of Christ for His Body's sake, the Church—until, in a very real sense, the language of the soul finds expression in the words of Paul the apostle: "As *dying*, and behold, we live; as *chastened*, and not killed; as *sorrowful*, yet always rejoicing; as *poor*, yet making many rich; as *having nothing*, and yet possessing all things" (2 Cor. 6:9–10). Like the Lord they serve, "*crucified* through weakness" (13:4)—daily, even hourly weakness—yet living, in union with Him as the Risen One, by the power of God toward others for whom He died.*

When later she was lunching with a group of speakers and ministers, she protested that she was "no theologian." The reply came immediately from one of the party: "You have the very best kind of theology—the theology of the Holy Ghost." How was such an understanding of Scripture and equipment for ministry brought about?

* At the same time as the Bridge of Allan Convention, which was the occasion of this meeting, Mrs. Penn-Lewis was engaged in writing her book *The Story of Job* and this quotation is the final paragraph of this book.

To understand this it is necessary to go back to the beginning, and to see if we can trace something of the development of her spiritual life. How instructive such beginnings, backgrounds and early growth can be!

Born on February 28, 1861, Jessie Jones was the oldest of her parents' eight children—being followed by four brothers, two sisters, and then another brother. She was brought up, as she herself put it, "in religious surroundings and in the lap of Calvinistic Methodism." Her grandfather; the Rev. Samuel Jones, was an eminent minister of that "connection," his main ministry being the building up of believers and his favorite theme "The Atonement." Her father was a civil and mining engineer in the little town of Neath, in South Wales, where her parents were very active in all kinds of church work. They kept open house for ministers and others engaged in the work of the denomination. Later, as the younger generation were more and more making English their language and the services in the Methodist Church were in Welsh, her parents, being on cordial terms with the local Anglican rector, decided that she should attend the Sunday School of St. David's Church; and later she joined the choir.

Very early she gave evidence of being an exceptionally clever child—walking at nine months. But because she was a sickly child, the family doctor forbade her being pressed in any way to learn. In spite of this she taught herself to read and at four years of age could read the Bible freely. She was able to pick up a story book and afterwards to describe every character in it. But the brake was applied to any thought of formal education until she was eight. Then she was sent to a boarding school for periods of about three months at a time, the other months being spent at farmhouses in the mountains, where there was no temptation to read and she could run wild in the country.

Even so, her home was a library of books, her father being a great buyer and reader of many classical and other standard works.

Being physically frail, she had to struggle against recurring illness all through life. This fact has to be kept in mind, for no true understanding of Jessie Penn-Lewis can be reached without remembering this handicap. A happy home; a father who was never too busy to find time for his children, was a delightful companion, and a stickler for truth being told and promises kept; books everywhere; the close proximity of open country and a garden where cricket was played and there were trees to climb-all these things were her joy in early years.

Then at ten years of age she was sent to a boarding school in Swansea, where special precautions were taken to care for her health; and it was here that she began to understand something of the limitations of her physical strength. She herself told of a pathetic incident when she crept into a boot cupboard and sobbed because the other children were sent out to play, but she had been kept in because an east wind was blowing; and it was not long before it was decided that she needed her mother's constant care and was returned home.

Mother and daughter were in this way thrown closely together, and she soon began to share her mother's interest in the cause of temperance. So keen a "Good Templar" did she become, in fact, that on the first lodge night after her twelfth birthday she was initiated into the adult lodge. Before long a junior lodge was opened, and she found an outlet for her gift of organization as presiding officer of this lodge, composed of forty to fifty children—the Treasurer being William Penn-Lewis (her future husband), then age fourteen.

At fourteen further "promotion" came to her, and she was made Honorary Secretary for the adult lodge, a friend of the family stepping in to give her some secretarial training. For quarter after quarter she was re-elected to this post, and she filled it with real enjoyment and efficiency until she was sixteen.

It was at this point that the family was called to face the sad loss of husband and father. After an illness of two years, Mr. Jones died in the prime of life and at a time of rising success in his profession. "My mother," wrote Mrs. Penn-Lewis later in life, "was left with eight children; I was the eldest, being sixteen, while the youngest was only three months old. How well I remember the funeral, when from a window I watched the sad procession, with two uncles behind the coffin and two fatherless boys on either side." Financial difficulties followed, and the widow gallantly faced her heavy responsibilities, be coming so successful in business that she was able to send one of the boys to Oxford, to send a second through training as a civil engineer, and the third as a surveyor, finally setting them all on their feet. So it was that Jessie Jones inherited from her parents a legacy of integrity, ability, courage, and perhaps above all, a capacity for sacrificial love.

At nineteen came her marriage to William Penn-Lewis, who had become Auditor's Clerk for the County of Sussex, which meant living in Brighton. Mr. Penn-Lewis was warned before the wedding by one of the bride's uncles that he was marrying one who was likely to be an invalid for life. This in no way deterred him, and he proved to be a constant source of strength, encouragement and support to her all through the active life of ministry to which God commissioned her.

Jessie spoke of her marriage as a "genuine love match." She loved William for his character. She reasoned that a man who never broke his word and never failed an appointment was a safe one to whom to trust her life.

As it often is with children brought up in the midst of religious surroundings, her true inward change of heart did not come until she had married and moved away from the old home. At the time of their marriage, William was attending the Church of the Annunciation at Brighton. Neither of them, however, threw themselves into the vicar's High Church teaching and practices.

Some eighteen months after her marriage she began to feel ill at ease about the Lord's Second Coming. She realized that she was not prepared to meet Him and really began to seek the Lord. It was at this point that she first glimpsed one of the great secrets of the Christian life: that she must deal with God Himself, direct and alone.

Would it not be true to say that every living biography you have read tells the same story? There comes a time when no human help can avail, and the influence of another personality can only be a disastrous hindrance. God is jealous in His love and will Himself reveal the salvation secured for us at such cost. He will not share His glory with another.

So it was that Mrs. Penn-Lewis wrote:

> My conversion occurred without the aid of any human instrument, but the day—New Year's Day, 1882—and the hour are imprinted on my mind. Only a deep desire to know that I was a child of God; a taking of my too-little-read Bible from the shelf; a turning over of the leaves, and my eye falling on the words, "*The Lord hath laid upon Him the iniquity of us all*"; again a casual turn of the sacred pages and the

> words, *"He that believeth hath eternal life."* A quick facing out whether I *did* believe that God had laid my sins upon the Lamb of God on the cross; a pause for wonderment that it really said that I had eternal life if I simply believed God's Word; a quick cry of, *"Lord, I do believe"*—and one more soul had passed from death to life, a trophy of the grace of God and the love of Him who died. The Spirit of God instantly bore witness with my spirit that I was a child of God, and deep peace filled my soul.

The immediate result of this transaction with God, and of His acceptance of one who, believing His promise, came to Him on the ground of Calvary alone, was a deepening consciousness of her own sinfulness. Jessie soon found that her at tempts to overcome her besetting sins ended in abject failure, and the succeeding few months were a record of bitter repentance and many tears over sins she was utterly unable to conquer.

One of the wonderful things in the Christian life is the way in which God, knowing the needs of His children, works on their behalf and brings them into touch with those who can help and guide just when they need it most. So it is fascinating to see Him opening the door for the next stage of the journey. In August of 1883, Mr. Penn-Lewis was appointed Borough Accountant of Richmond in Surrey, where they found their way to Holy Trinity Church and came under the ministry of Rev. Evan H. Hopkins, who has been called the theologian of the early Keswick Conventions. The very first sermon was "an opening of heaven" to the intense and hungry heart of Jessie Penn-Lewis. For the first time she heard of the way of victory over besetting sins through the blood of Christ, of the joy of a full surrender to Him, and the possibilities of a Spirit-filled life.

One day when Jessie was visiting the vicarage, Mrs. Hopkins asked her a direct question as to whether she was "a Christian." Her immediate reply was "Yes," and this was her first open confession of Christ. Another question followed—"Did she know victory over sin?" And she had to admit that she had "never heard of it." But there was in her heart a longing for the utmost that God could do for her, and her innate honesty prevented her from being content with anything less.

Jessie's pursuit of the goal she sought in the face of the physical weakness which was a constant handicap to her is best glimpsed in her own words. A half-sheet of notepaper dated 8 a.m., February 28th, 1884, gives us an insight into God's dealings with her and hers with Him.

> Lord Jesus, on this my 23rd birthday I do again yield my whole self unto Thee, soul and spirit, life, time, hands, feet, eyes, lips, voice, money, intellect, will, heart, love, health, thoughts and desires. All that I have, all that I am, all that I may be is Thine, wholly, absolutely and unreservedly. And I do believe that Thou dost take me, and that Thou wilt work in me to *will* and

> to *do* Thy good pleasure. Lord, use me in whatever way it seemeth good to Thee, keep my eyes fixed on Thee, ready to obey even Thy glance. Thou art my King, my Saviour, and my Guide. Take not Thy Holy Presence from me, but day by day draw me nearer, until that glorious time when I shall see Thee face to face, and faith be lost in sight. Amen.

An entry in her tiny pocket diary made after a watch night service as the year 1886 opened runs: "Thank God, I commence the year 'right with Him,' but I long intensely to be more single-eyed to His glory, my will more lost in His."

Another series of entries read:

> A day of constant temptation and battle against a discontented spirit. Was enabled to hold on all through in spite of darkness: Fear I gave way many times, but was kept near to the precious Blood. . . . Gave way once or twice to hasty speaking. Oh, how I want even the tone of my voice to be gentle. Am more at peace and trusting, but still not very bright, but I mean to keep on trusting. . . . Very tired all day, felt ruffled again this morning. When shall I learn the peace and love that endureth all things and is not easily provoked! Difficult to believe afterwards that the Lord *does* forgive at once, so depression instead of fullness of joy fills one's soul. One wants to *feel* forgiven—how much training one needs, and how patient the Lord is!

How good He is to those who seek to follow Him! There were also, of course, times of deep conscious fellowship with the Lord she was growing to know more closely, and entries read: "Happy day, no cloud, but conscious presence and smile of the Lord—oh, why do I not trust Him more utterly in times of temptation? . . . Happy day again, the Lord so near and so precious. Such sweet sense of nothing between."

It was about this time that Mr. Penn-Lewis found the Lord Jesus Christ as his Saviour and Lord. What joy this gave her!

And from then on they sought together to serve Him and win others to Him. Those were busy days. Mr. Penn-Lewis soon became a powerful speaker in open air meetings; and a mission held in Richmond in March of 1886 gave both great opportunities for personal work.

Many of us will recognize in these brief extracts from her diary the joys and testings of our own early efforts in His service.

> Led two children to Jesus and had a long talk with young B_____. He yielded so far as to promise me to go home and pray God to give him the desire.
>
> At Hammond's meeting, although poorly all day. Young B_____ there: I watched for him. . . . After a long time, thank God, he decided. . . . I was led to *claim* him this afternoon.

> Spoke to Walter D_____, but no good—Lord have mercy on him!
>
> At College Hall this afternoon—led four boys to decision.

"Young B_____" appears to have been very really "born again," for later on we find him speaking at a meeting, followed by the note, "Thank God, he is coming on well!"

And through it all there appears a little refrain of the young wife's practical daily round: "Very busy all day—making marmalade, ironing, etc."

What happy, formative years in His school those must have been, preparing both husband and wife for all that was to follow in. His plan for them!

CHAPTER TWO

WORKING FOR GOD

IT is not an easy lesson for any young Christian to learn that there is all the difference in the world between our working *for* God and His working *through* us. So it was with Jessie Penn-Lewis. God was quietly preparing her for the time when the promise of John 7:38 could be fulfilled and He would be able to pour out through her the "rivers of living water."

Jessie was now librarian and a committee member of the Rescue Home for Girls; she also was conducting a Bible class at the Home on Sunday afternoons. She flung herself into the work with characteristic intensity and found many opportunities for personal work among the girls.

On one occasion she took one of the girls into her own home as a maid, but after causing considerable trouble the girl "ran away with a soldier." Undaunted, Mrs. Penn-Lewis, accompanied by the matron of the Home, set out on a three days' search at a number of centers where soldiers were stationed; but the search proved fruitless, and she reached home at midnight "dead beat." This was typical of her concern for those in need.

The year 1889 proved to be one of constant illness, and her diary entries are one long story of pain and weakness caused by pleurisy and lung trouble, which was growing worse. But there was no slackening in the work she had undertaken. Long committee meetings in connection with the Rescue Home, gatherings for prayer and Bible classes were bravely persevered with in spite of the resulting physical exhaustion. There were also now daily interviews with girls seeking spiritual help, all calling for special prayer and thought; and each name was noted in her diary.

During the previous year she had greatly missed a very close friend who had been long absent from Richmond. It was now clear that the Lord was leading His child deeper down into fellowship with Himself in preparation for the ministry for which He Himself was equipping her. On the last night of the old year (1888) a longer note than usual tells how both ladies recognized His schooling at this time.

> Such a sweet talk with X_____ over the lessons our souls had learned in our separation. She found she had learned more of Christ, and I knew the same. I discovered that I had been longing for human companionship in the pressing on, and I saw that I must be content to be

> *alone* in soul if I would press on to the heights. I remembered the picture of "The Broad and Narrow Way" and the number of people just beyond the cross, and the *ones* and *twos* pressing on to the heights beyond. I remembered even Jesus was lonely in soul, and I saw that if I would press on I must be content to be lonely too, as far as other people go. Content to press on with Jesus alone as my Companion. As soon as I saw this, I saw what had, in a manner, kept me lingering about. Now I will not linger any longer but follow Jesus right ahead.

The fact is, of course, that God is jealous in His love and will not have us rely on any fellowship which would threaten to rival His own. If He allowed us to lean on human props too greatly, He could never teach us those lessons we need to master if we are to lead others safely to Him. Possibly the greatest need we have is that of learning to go to Him *first* at all times.

An important moment in her spiritual life came now, exactly timed as the Lord's provision always is for those who are seeking Him and His plan for their lives. The book *The Spirit of Christ* by Dr. Andrew Murray was given to her and was devoured. A snowy Sunday in February was spent reading Murray's devotional study. "It seems so deep, and almost beyond comprehension, but I do so long to know more of it. I seem to know so little—may He teach me!" Ten days later the diary records her joy at the fresh light on the working of the Holy Spirit that was coming to her. In reference to the book, she wrote:

> I came on the words "To others it comes as a deep, quiet, but clearer insight into the fullness of the Spirit of Christ as being theirs, and a faith that feels confident that His sufficiency is equal to every emergency." These words fairly "lit up" to me, and I saw that this had been my experience lately. I have *never* seen His power as I see it now. . . . Has not Jesus been teaching me knowledge, love, and obedience these last years; and have I not been entering into the fellowship of His death this winter as never before? Have I not been seeing the hopelessness of the flesh and feeling keenly its utter insufficiency?

New light was in such ways being given, but as yet there was no steady victory over what she felt to be her besetting sins. The chief of these was the hasty spirit which was part of her Welsh inheritance, and fuel was added to it by physical weakness and exhaustion. But this was never allowed to minimize a fault in her own eyes. After nearly a week, for instance, of spring-cleaning, with workmen in the house and long hours of household sewing, with interviews, meetings and other activities sandwiched in between, she recorded in her diary: "So worn out at night. Some bitter falls through physical exhaustion—yet inexcusable!"

During the spring a serious cough developed, accompanied by high temperatures at night, and she went to the seaside for a spell, being too ill to do much more than lie about in the sun or go for short drives. She lost weight rapidly and for the first time coughed up a little blood. At times it seemed as if her frail life was ebbing away. Returning to Richmond, she picked up her work again, but November and December found her once again on the South Coast.

All through this period the unremitting search for deliverance from sin and fear, and for equipment for service, was pursued—and God was leading her and deepening His work in her. One Sunday in December she attended a service in Eastbourne and went up to the penitent form for deliverance from self-consciousness, but the degree of liberty experienced as a result was neither great nor lasting. And yet, through the increasing bodily weakness, a necessary lesson was gradually being understood. She needed to learn to take Christ's life and strength for her body when engaged in His service. Physical healing was not given and the consumptive symptoms persisted, but one bitterly cold day in February of 1890 there was this revealing entry in her diary: "In all day; then claimed of the Lord strength and physical keeping, and went to my Bible class at the Rescue Home . . . came home tired, but happy and thankful."

But the gift she had asked for was sought for service, not for herself; for on the following day, the wind being still easterly, the entry runs:

"Stayed in all day . . . am no worse for last night, but felt I could not ask God to keep me if I went out today needlessly. So against my inclination, I stayed in."

Soon after this, in March, came a call to undertake the position of Honorary Secretary of the Richmond YWCA, and with—humanly speaking—only a few months to live, Mrs. Penn-Lewis ventured to accept it. She pleaded with her doctor that, seeing she had likely but a brief span of life before her, he might allow her to "die doing something for God." She immediately threw herself enthusiastically into this new sphere of service. She organized a musical drill, singing classes, shorthand lessons—anything, in fact, that would be likely to draw the girls of the town into contact with the gospel. Once again her own words express more clearly than anyone else possibly could her reading of the work done during this period.

> After a time I became conscious that the spiritual results were not equivalent to the labor of the work. I began to question whether I knew the *fullness* of the Holy Spirit. Without doubt I had received Him and had "entered into rest" as concerned my own life and fellowship with God: But when I compared the small results of my service with the fruit given to the apostles at Pentecost, I could not but own that I did not know the Holy Spirit in the fullness of His power.

> My weekly Bible class was a great trouble to me, for I had no power of utterance. Organizing work was much easier, but meetings were a sore trial. Self-consciousness almost paralyzed me, and no practice ever made speaking less difficult. Others might have the gift of speech, but it was clearly not given to me, I said. So all the people whom I could discover who were filled with the Spirit I invited to Richmond. Everyone I heard of who knew anything about the Holy Spirit, I asked to come and speak to my girls—I was so anxious that they should get this blessing. I settled it in my mind that I was not the channel. I was not the one to speak. Until one day the Lord turned on me and said: *Why NOT yourself? These people have quite enough to do without coming to do YOUR work! Why NOT you the channel?* But, I said, I cannot speak! It takes me a whole day to prepare for my class: What can I do? It is impossible!

Outwardly a most successful work was going on, but Mrs. Penn-Lewis could not feel satisfied. She knew in her heart of hearts her lack of power; and God was quietly leading her on. And again her own words tell the story best.

> I came to an end of my own energy and strength. How I taught the girls in my Bible class! How *full* my Bible was of notes, and how carefully I prepared a dish of spiritual food for them! "Food" all obtained secondhand, from other books. But they did not change much in their lives.

> I thought it was the fault of the girls, until the Lord spoke to me and said, "*It is yourself!*" "But Lord, I am consecrated! What can it be in me? I give time every morning to read and pray: I have put everything right in my life as far as I know." But the Lord still said "*It is YOU*." And then He began to break me, and there came to me the terrible revelation that every bit of this activity, this energy, this indomitable perseverance, was *myself* after all, though it was hidden under the name of "consecration."

This first unveiling of self-life led, early in 1892, to the little band of workers connected with the YWCA Institute meeting weekly to wait upon God definitely for an enduement of power and an outpouring of the Holy Spirit upon the work. As they prayed they were clearly shown that there was a work of God to be done in *themselves* before the outpouring could come upon the Institute. Mrs. Penn-Lewis herself read book after book upon the subject of the Holy Spirit, searching to find out whether God did actually promise His children as full an indwelling and outworking of the Spirit as in the days of Pentecost—only to find herself more and more confused by the differing teachings of the various "schools of thought." Finally, she wrote:

> I said, I will go straight to God and ask Him to prove to me whether there is *for me* an enduement for service that will liberate me in utterance as it did Peter at Pentecost. I will put it to

the proof for myself! Away went the books, and away went the various views and theories. In desperation I said I WILL GO TO GOD.

From this time I never admitted another question but set myself with steady determination to prove for myself if there was anything in it. Then slowly, as I held on to God, there grew within me a deepening purpose that at all costs I would obtain this enduement for service; until at last there came such a cry to God for it, as the supreme thing I wanted, that I could say He might take away all things from me if He would only answer this cry. It was a long time before it got to that, but it brought about such an absolute surrender of my will to God that I have never had to fight a battle of surrender of will from that time. I could say He should do absolutely what He liked with my life if He would only give me that liberation of the Holy Spirit that Peter knew at Pentecost.

Peter was the pattern I put before the Lord. I saw that Peter was not "nervous" that day, and I intensely felt my great need was to be delivered from an over powering nervousness and a kind of paralysis in speech that fairly mastered me. I cried, "I want the deliverance that Peter got at Pentecost. I do not care what other Christians call it. If 'the baptism of the Spirit' is not the right term, give me the right words to use. I do not care about the words, but *I want the thing*."

> In this way I held on to God with an intensity which caused "people" to fall away from my mind, with all they said about this great liberation for service which I was seeking. Then a deep rest came into me that God would do what I had asked, and I could wait His way and time.
>
> Thus I learned the true meaning of "waiting" for "the promise of the Father." I had reached a quiet attitude of dependence upon God, that He would answer my cry in *His own time*. Then I went on with my usual work, not in indifference, but with a steady hold of faith that some time the enduement would come. But I was sorely tested. My experience after that was a deeper, and deeper, and deeper sense of failure. Everything seemed to be worse and worse, instead of better and better as I had thought it would be after such a tremendous transaction with God. I appeared to lose all I already had. I grew worse and worse in nervousness and "horror" in speaking to my Bible class, and everything seemed failure.*

One outcome of this keen searching of heart and intense desire to know more of the Holy Spirit's power was a ten-day mission held at the Institute in February 1892 by Miss H.E. Soltau, of the China Inland Mission. Bible readings for

---

*This was incorporated into her booklet *Power for Service*.

ladies were held in the afternoons, and meetings for members of the YWCA and others in the evenings, including two Sundays. It was something of a shock to the Secretary when, after the first evening meeting, Miss Soltau said to her: "I must send to London for someone to come here to pray, for this place is like a *wall*! There is no break-there is not enough prayer to move it." "*A wall*!" And the Secretary and organizer had been so proud of her "consecrated branch"!

She said, in speaking years afterwards of this time:

> I thought there was no YWCA branch in the country like it. I had talked of consecration to the members and we *had* consecrated ourselves. It shows how easy it is to get things into our heads and not have them in our lives! "No break"? I could not understand what she meant. But she said a "break" was needed, so I stood back and watched—until at last I saw souls broken down through that broken messenger and many coming to Christ. By the end of the week *there was a break*—souls were being saved at every meeting, and I said, "Is this what you call a break?" It was an education to me!

From this point the meetings increased in power and interest, until at the praise meeting, which closed the mission, the rooms at the Institute were crowded out, and nearly forty testimonies to definite blessing were sent in, together with thank-offerings of money and jewelry.

After this practical illustration of what "the enduement of power from on high" might mean, the "furnace of intense desire" for such an enduement increased. "Do for me what You did for Peter at Pentecost," she prayed again, as she felt more and more keenly her lack of "utterance" and the bondage of self-consciousness. Then the Spirit of God began to question her, and to bring to light the "thoughts and intents" of her heart.

Again the story comes better in her own words:

> Then two or three searching questions were put to me by the Spirit of God. The first was: "*If I answer your cry, are you willing to be unpopular?*" UNPOPULAR! Be rejected? Well yes, I am willing. I have never faced it before, but I am willing.
>
> "*Why do you desire the fullness of the Spirit?*" Was it for success in service, and that I should be considered a much-used worker? Would I desire the same fullness of the Spirit if it meant apparent failure, and becoming the off-scouring of all things in the eyes of others? This had not occurred to me before, and I quickly agreed to any conditions the Lord should please to set before me. Again came the question "*Will you be willing to have no great experience, but agree to live and walk entirely by faith in the Word of God?*" But I said, "I thought people who had enduement of power always had an experience! Did not Finney and Asa Mahan?" How am I to

know I have had it if I do not get an experience? "*Are you willing to walk in bare faith on My Word, and never have any wonderful experience?*" YES! These were the questions put to me by God, and there the matter dropped.

Then came the climax, when one morning I awoke and saw before me a hand holding up in terrible light a handful of filthy rags, while a gentle voice said: "*This is the outcome of all your past service for God.*" "But Lord, I have been surrendered and consecrated to Thee all these years; it was consecrated work!" "*Yes, My child, but all your service has been CONSECRATED SELF; the outcome of your OWN ENERGY; your OWN PLANS for winning souls; your OWN DEVOTION. All for Me, I grant you, but* yourself, *all the same.*" The unveiling was truly a horror to me, and brought me in deep abasement to the blood of Christ for cleansing. Then came the still, small voice once more, and this time it was the one little word "CRUCIFIED!"

Crucified—What did it mean? I had not asked to be *crucified* but to be *filled*. But now Romans 6:6–11 became a power to me, and I knew the meaning of our "old man was crucified with Him" and what Paul meant in His words, "crucified with Christ" (Gal. 2:20).

As a little child, I rested on the word thus given, and then it "pleased the Lord to reveal His Son in me that I might preach Him"—I knew the Risen Lord.

Often in the Psalms a paragraph needing to be underlined closes with the word *Selah*. One of the best paraphrases of this word is perhaps "Stop and think"; and I wonder if that is not exactly what we should do now. How closely this last sentence harmonizes with the Lord's own promise given in John 16:14—"*He shall glorify Me*"; and the seeker's immediate response was "*I knew the Risen Lord.*" We are to proclaim *Him*, not an experience. An acid test to any claim to be filled with the Spirit is "Is the Lord Jesus Christ given the preeminent place?"

There is one other point that emerges, which has been expressed in this way: "Calvary precedes Pentecost. Death with Christ precedes the fullness of the Holy Spirit. *Power*! Yes, God's children need power, *but God does not give power to the old creation nor to the uncrucified soul*. Some may have a *measure* of power, *but not what God wants to give*. Satan will give power to the 'old Adam' *but God will not.*"

This revelation of the Risen Lord—the first drops of the showers which were to become a very river of "waters to swim in"—came suddenly and unexpectedly, not in an hour of "waiting upon God" nor in a meeting with others seeking the same blessing, but at the breakfast table in her own home one morning in March, 1892. The glory of the Lord was revealed in her spirit with such blinding power that she fled to her own room to fall upon her knees in worship and speechless adoration. Her own summary of this enduement is worth careful study. She wrote:

> 1. It was sudden, and when I was not specially thinking about the matter.
> 2. I knew in my spirit that He had come.
> 3. My Bible became like a living thing and was flooded with light.
> 4. Christ suddenly became to me a real Person: I could not explain how knew, but He became real to me.
> 5. When I went to my Bible class, I found myself able to speak with liberty of utterance, with the conviction of the Spirit at the back of it, until souls were convicted of sin on every side.
> 6. There was power in prayer, so that it seemed I only needed to ask and have.
> 7. My spirit took its way to God, freed from every fetter that held to anything on earth.

Once again we shall do well to let her continue the story in her own words.

> For three months I lived in a very heaven of joy and light and gladness, and the very name of Jesus was so sweet that the sound of it caused me to melt into tears and to be filled with exquisite joy. Then came the gradual cessation of the heavenly experience, and the time of danger. I began to dread the loss of my experience and to seek anew that which seemed to be slipping from me. At this point I was shown,

by the mercy of God, the path of the cross, and the wisdom of God in withdrawing the *gifts* of God for the soul to rest entirely in Him and not in joy or ecstatic communion—which made me spiritually self-absorbed and apt to pity others not on my plane of spiritual life. I wanted only to be left alone to retire within for communion with my Beloved. But when I saw that the loss of this spiritual delight and ecstasy meant fruit, through death and a life *in God Himself* above His gifts, I gladly chose the path of the cross and consented to walk in the night—of faith to that goal where God would be All in All.

Through depth after depth of fellowship with the Christ in His death did the Lord Himself lead me in succeeding years, until my vision cleared and cleared, to see that the cross of Calvary was the very pivot of all things, and was the one great supply to the need of the child of God in every aspect of his spiritual life. And I saw that, after all, that which I had thought was *the goal* of the Christian life was really meant by the Lord to be but the beginning of a path which should lead into the fellowship of the cross and into union with the Ascended Lord in the bosom of the Father. The secret of a fruitful life is, in brief, to pour out to others, *and want nothing for yourself*—to leave your self utterly in the hands of God and not care what happens *to you.*

CHAPTER 3

GOD AT WORK

ON the day of Pentecost the little band who had made the upper room their meeting place in which to prepare for the promised advent of the Holy Spirit were brought triumphantly out into a realm where God Himself was engaged in a new work among men. Those disciples had no time to settle down into a self-conscious enjoyment of the amazing experience that was now theirs. They were carried forward on wave after wave of activity and an outpouring of blessing to those in need around them. The most casual reading of the early chapters of what Dr. A.T. Pierson called "The Acts of the Holy Spirit" will again and again bring out the truth of this statement.

As it was then, so it was now in the life of Jessie Penn-Lewis. Immediately the living waters broke out in a flood-tide of blessing to others. In private talks, classes and meetings, the presence and power of God were such that scarcely a soul went away untouched by Him. Many passed from death to life, some being convicted of sin without being spoken to, and numbers of God's own children were led to fuller surrender of heart and life, realizing and entering into "the exceeding greatness of His power" to save *to the uttermost.*

To come over the threshold of the Richmond Institute was to come into the felt presence of God, and many stepped down into the river of blessing without the touch of any human instrument. The prayer meetings were now times of great liberty and rejoicing in free access to the Throne of Grace. In the past they had so often been lacking in liberty that the Secretary, in her earnest longing that her girls should learn to pray aloud, would sometimes put slips of paper with little prayers written upon them on the chairs of those she felt ought to join in audible prayer! No need now to toil to arouse missionary interest, for in this atmosphere of the Spirit of God hearts were enlarged to receive the passion of Christ for the salvation of the world, and prayer was made that the living waters flowing among them might reach to the ends of the earth.

These prayers were abundantly answered later on by the Lord scattering many of the members as missionaries to various parts of the world. One such wrote from India early in 1893.

> God is doing great things for me! I could hardly believe that the things you told me could really

> be true, but indeed God is working as great miracles here! All day long and nearly every day, I am dealing in some way or another with souls. I can see God is speaking to the hearts of the headmistresses in some of the chief schools. God has filled my own heart with such joy that people are astonished, and I really think it is the joy that attracts them.

So the "upper room" at the Richmond Institute became a sanctuary from whence the rivers flowed in every direction, and calls poured in upon Mrs. Penn-Lewis to carry the message of this more abundant life to other places in Great Britain.*

A "Ready Band" was formed among the girls—ready for any manner of service and the Sunday night gospel meeting, started during Miss Soltau's mission and held after the usual evening

---

*It is perhaps remarkable that one of the earliest requests for outside meetings was to visit both Brighton and Eastbourne, where she had earlier been sent to be nursed. Of these meetings the diary record says: "It was just as if the people had been soaked in a life tide from heaven! It was not a case of individual blessing—the people were *all* submerged in a flood-tide of life from God which quickened them, released them, and brought them out into a new life. I did not need to speak personally to them, there seemed nothing to do but to give the mes sage as God gave it to me, and the Holy Ghost did the rest. From that hour I understood, and knew intelligently that it was *dying* not *doing* that produced spiritual fruit."

service in the churches, became the opportunity for members to engage in the work of seeking to reach the young girls who thronged the streets of Richmond on Sunday evening "fishing" it was called. Many of these were brought in, and souls were led to Christ week after week, who, in their turn became fishers also.

God also touched the financial side of the work, and Mrs. Penn-Lewis learned a lesson which molded her attitude toward finance for the entire period of her life of service. Afterwards she was always certain that if God wanted a thing carried through, He would provide the necessary means. And she was always ready to drop anything, however fruitful it had been, should He show, by withholding His hand, that the thing was "finished" in His plan and purpose. In connection with the Institute she had been in the habit of collecting subscriptions for the work, but now she had to tell the committee that she could no longer use this method. God must move His people to give and thereby supply the needs of His own work.

So, as needs arose, they were laid before the Heavenly Father—and many were the romances of answered prayer. On one occasion the Institute's stock of coal had run out—barely sufficient was left for a fire that day—and the resident worker had not mentioned it, for she knew there were no funds in hand. But she and another knelt in the empty coal house and cried to the Lord that He would send the needed supply. That day an anonymous letter was dropped into the letter box. Enclosed was a small card with a golden sovereign fastened on and the words “COALS, YWCA.” What rejoicing there was! And what strengthening of their faith to ask and expect that all their needs would be met in due course! At other times the money poured in so fast that it was difficult to keep a record of the items.

“What,” you may ask, “of the spiritual liberty and power of utterance asked for?” The diary tells of “blessed freedom,” of power with others never known before, of messages given without a tremor of the self-conscious misery of the past. The first test came the week following Jessie’s experience of the Spirit’s fullness. As Thursday drew near, and with it the Bible class at the Rescue Home which had often caused her so much suffering and such intense strain, the entry in the diary for this day (March 24th, 1892) reads: “My testing day! Trusted for message, and used no help! Mrs._____ was there, but I was kept in perfect peace.”

And of the same evening at the Institute, she wrote: “Still victory! Went to class fully trusting. Between fifty and sixty there, and intense power, full liberty and full joy—it was glorious!”

From this particular meeting there was real fruit. During the next few days one and another came for talks—two hard backsliders were brought back, sobbing, to the Saviour’s feet; a fellow worker sought "the anointing," and another rejoiced in full surrender—the last link was snapped. So, one by one, her fellow workers came into the same liberty and joy.

On March 25th, Mrs. Evan Hopkins wrote:

> I rejoice with you that you are fully in the stream and the stream in you. Glorious indeed is this anointing! Where will it end? "Waters to swim in"—no little trickling rivulet—"Ye have an unction." This is the positive part of the blessing. Cleansing and keeping are only the preparation: The anointing abideth and continueth ever more and more, if we do not hinder; then we may expect a continuous inflow and outflow. We have plunged in, we are no longer standing on the brink, and now comes the willing, joyous giving out to others, and "everything shall live whither the river cometh." . . .
>
> No more "I can't"—what a change! He can, *He can*, HE CAN! May the Lord bring many more to hunger! He only makes them hunger to satisfy and fill. Blessed, blessed it is to know this! It is worth going through the hunger and the death in order to get such a blessing.

Pages might be filled with records of the wonderful way that God was working, not only in the activities of the Institute but through the witness of the members themselves in many areas of the life of the community. The yearly attendances at the various classes increased from 6,900 to nearly

13,000 during the three years which followed the movement of the Spirit of God; and it seemed that at every meeting there was definite blessing. People came from many different areas, seeking to learn the secret of this rising tide of life, and went away rejoicing in a similar anointing of the Holy Spirit. Visitors dropping in for only one evening met with the Lord and found deliverance from many a yoke of bondage. This work in no way centered around the workers but was wholly from the presence of God in the midst. There was an intense sense of the Lord's presence, and the workers had to learn to stand aside and watch Him deal with souls Himself.

It seemed as if every member became a worker, and they were grouped into bands for various types of service. There was, for instance, a register kept of the various Sunday schools in the town needing temporary teachers, and nearly one hundred of these classes were supplied with volunteers from the YWCA.

As so often happens when the Spirit is at work, one of the members felt a very clear call to His service (and we should perhaps remind ourselves here that such a call does not always send us out into the forefront of activity and leadership). Mary Tugwell, already an experienced cook, left her position with a wealthy family and offered her services to help Mrs. Penn-Lewis in the home. Here she fulfilled a valuable ministry for many years, being able to set Mrs. Penn-Lewis free from household cares to move out unencumbered into the wider ministry which was opening before her. She became housekeeper, nurse, and trusted friend whose deep, understanding fellowship was a great strength in the years ahead.

Over the same period that God poured out such blessing at Richmond, He was graciously at work in other places of Christian work and witness. The Geelong Convention—Australia—held in the autumn of 1891, had been an occasion for a movement of the Spirit of God which spread far and wide. Its influence was felt at the Keswick Convention of 1892, which proved to be one of the most remarkable of those early conventions. The vision of the cross was central in all this movement of the Spirit. Mr. George Soltau wrote of the Geelong Convention:

> I wish to bear my testimony that it was nothing less than the fullness of the Spirit. We were drunk with the joy of the Lord and with the vistas of the possibilities of faith opening up to the fully surrendered life of the believer. But it was equally manifest to us all that this joy and blessing is only to be received, and retained, and increased, by the death to self and of self, and the most painful crucifixion of self (see Gal. 5:24).

But we must return to Richmond! The work of bringing girls to Christ and quickening Christians into new life continued steadily. Then in the report of the YWCA for 1894/1895 Mrs. Penn-Lewis wrote:

> Each year in some way has its own characteristics, and this last year will be known as one of scattering, after three years of ceaseless reaping through the manifest presence of the Eternal Spirit in our midst. Early in 1895 we were led to pray definitely that God would scatter His children whom He saw to be ripe for His use in other places, and He quickly took us at our word.

There followed a steady exodus of members all over England into all kinds of work and witness, one of them becoming Secretary of another large Richmond branch. Perhaps one of the most unexpected developments was the thrusting out of the resident worker of the branch to missionary work in South Africa, taking one of the other members with her.

This seems to be the inevitable pattern of any special work of the Spirit. It was an incredibly short time after the day of Pentecost when, we read of the believers in Jerusalem: "They were scattered abroad and went everywhere preaching the word" (Acts 8:4). The result of this scattering was, "And the hand of the Lord was with them: and a great number believed, and turned unto the Lord." The wisdom of the flesh says "Build up!" The wisdom of the Spirit says "Scatter."

Mrs. Penn-Lewis herself paid a visit to her hometown—Neath—and blessing resulted. A branch of the YWCA was started, which grew into a sturdy work in its own right. This led to the first special mission to young women ever held in the town. She wrote of this mission:

> Night after night the girls thronged in, and souls were swept into the Kingdom! The presence of God was so manifest that every barrier was broken down: Numbers broke into prayer in the meetings and, when asked to go into another room to be dealt with, would stream in and before each other kneel and yield to Christ. There has been no hesitation in boldly confessing Christ in their homes and business houses: Five girls in one shop are rejoicing together; another young Christian from last year now rejoices over two sisters gathered in. It was blessed to see the converts of the night before bringing their friends to be led to Christ and taking them to the prayer room.
>
> The anniversary tea which closed the week's mission was held in a large hall lent us for the occasion; over 200 sat down to tea, and then we had a three-hour meeting for praise and testimony. Numbers rose to their feet to confess their new-found Saviour. Not only the young converts testified, but numbers of God's own children, to whom God had revealed the glorious secret of "*Christ in you*," the only power for life and service. When all who had received definite blessing were asked to rise, about 180 rose—and we sang "What a Wonderful Saviour Is Jesus, My Jesus!"

> As we closed this blessed anniversary and praise meeting, all the unsaved who desired to seek Christ were asked to go into the vestry, and numbers instantly rose and pressed in. It was a glorious ingathering that night. In addition, forty new members were enrolled.

The hallmark of a genuine work of the Spirit is that as it grows it is not dependent on man: God continues to provide leadership for it in His own way. So it was that both at Richmond and Neath the leadership passed to others, and God opened wider doors of service for His servant. But that must be the theme of the next chapter.

We must remember that the work of the Spirit we have been looking at was almost entirely among young people. Is there anything we can learn from this fact? Later in life Mrs. Penn-Lewis was sharing in an open conference dealing with the growing trend to superficiality among young people. Her contribution not only gives us some understanding of her thinking but will well repay prayerful thought as it is read.

> In our YWCA we had all kinds of social activities—but when God came in, no one wanted them, and girls came who had said they would never come to the Institute! What is needed is the *positive influx* of the Spirit of God to fill the churches, and that God shall do such a deep work *in us* that there shall be a stronger force of life flowing out to others. I think that if a person goes to the theatre there is an inner craving for

something lacking, but it is misdirected. It is natural to want *life*, and all these things point to unsatisfied souls crying out for "life." I do not think we can condemn them—they must get "life" somewhere—but can't we give them life? There is a vacant place, an inward necessity, in everyone that nothing but the cross of Christ will satisfy; and if you recognize that, you will be able to give your witness without condemning others. We need to recognize that deep down in every human being there is a capacity for God, and these souls will never find rest until they find their rest in God.

I am intensely sympathetic with young folk when they see the old folk somberly plodding off to prayer meeting! Have you no sympathy? Would *you* have gone? That is what drew me into work among young girls. I had such sympathy with them. They want *life*, and if we do not give them the right kind of life, they will get the wrong kind. We need *life* in our churches, *life* in the prayer meetings, *life* everywhere! "How shall we get the young people into the churches?" Give them *life*—life from God.

In our YWCA Institute, we used to have souls saved even at our sale of work! I went down to Neath and helped to start a YWCA branch there, and God moved in the town. I remember at that first meeting we got together all the Neath ladies we could, and we gave a tea—my little mother and I. We gathered about seventy girls out of the shops and the ladies played games with them! At eight o'clock I said, "Girls, *we are going to pray*." In an instant there was quiet, and we led many of these girls to Christ that night. The Spirit of the Lord fell upon that meeting—I am sure I took six of them at a time and led them to the Lord.

But you will never help young people if you do not love them. I do so long that God's people will be more *human,* have more heart—cleansed heart, with Christ in it. You can do anything with people you love, and who love you. This is not *natural* love, because it loves the ugly and the unpleasant. It is the "love of God shed abroad in our hearts" that is needed. We are too occupied with our own spiritual growth and progress. "Oh, God, let us die to ourselves! Lord, come Thou and live in us, so that Thy life can flow out to others through us!"

CHAPTER 4

GOD'S PLAN UNFOLDS

THE Bible is packed with marvels, one of which is the way God loves us each one as an individual and plans for us in a way that no earthly father has ever planned for his children. What a thrilling verse Ephesians 2:10 is! "For God has made us what we are, created in Christ Jesus to do those good deeds *which He planned for us to do*" (J.B. Phillips). This was the practical discovery which the fullness of the Spirit enabled Mrs. Penn-Lewis to grasp and seek to live by.

In the spring of 1895 an invitation came to her from Miss Soltau, head of the Missionary Training Home of the China Inland Mission—now the Overseas Missionary Fellowship—to give the message at the Good Friday devotions meetings at Mildmay. She gave a brief summary from Scripture of the subjective teaching of the believer's death with Christ, a matter which the Holy Spirit was opening up to her as the basis of life and ministry. An outline of the message was taken down in longhand and sent out as a circular both to missionaries in China and workers at home. A friend who read it asked permission to print it in booklet form, and Mrs. Penn-Lewis filled in the outline. It was issued with the title *The Pathway to Life in God.* The first edition was soon sold out, and within five years 32,000 had been printed. The reason? A writer in *The Life of Faith* magazine gives the answer as clearly as possible: "A most valuable part of her teaching is about the detailed individual working of the Holy Ghost in the soul of the surrendered believer, holding it firm, guiding it in thought, feeling and action; reaching down into its secret sources—'All my springs are in Thee.' This is an important side of sanctification which is rarely dealt with."

This little booklet was appreciated by many Christian workers all over the world. A typical glimpse of its usefulness is given in a letter from Mr. J .H. Smeeton, an accountant in one of the great London banks who afterwards, at the age of 62, went out to Algiers to work among the blind beggars there.

> Though, as I told you, I had a sight of the death to "self" and of life in the Risen One, and was able by faith to recognize that I had a share in both, yet my experience was very limited. . . . I have often been utterly powerless to speak to souls even when they looked to me for a

> word, and my life appears to be nothing but a humbling and breaking down. Your pathway has given me the key to my problems, and my prayer has been, and is, "Lower, Lord, lower still." Seeing that from the helplessness of the grave it must be that God raises from the dead, I find I have been waiting for a resurrection experience which does not come by waiting but by faith.

Now, many decades later, the ministry of this little booklet still continues!

At times God's purpose for us seems slow to unfold, at others it seems to move at almost breathtaking speed—and yet so quietly and without stress! In March 1896 Mr. Penn-Lewis was appointed Treasurer to the Corporation of Leicester. A move now became inevitable. The Richmond era was brought to an end. Then within a month of the removal to Leicester, the first call to travel overseas for ministry came to Mrs. Penn-Lewis. This meant that a major decision faced them both. Look at the facts. In the first place, long, weary months of separation opened up before them. Then there was Mrs. Penn-Lewis' health. Could her husband allow her to face the strain of such a program? Remember also that those were days before air travel was dreamed of. Long journeys by sea and train were time-consuming and not always comfortable. Some paragraphs from a letter written at that time reveal something of the completeness of the surrender of both husband and wife to the Lord whom they loved and sought to serve. Mrs. Penn-Lewis wrote:

> My life is not my own. I can do nothing else but be obedient to the heavenly vision—since God has chosen the foolish things to confound the wise. Here am I, raised from the grave to be His instrument! Here am I to be spent, every breath, for the God who gives me breath. Our home is not our own, it is God's. We have nothing, we glory in being the slaves of Jesus Christ, my dear one and I. How we bless God for His grace to the chief of sinners! What glory it is to suffer all things lest we should hinder the Gospel of Christ!
>
> What selfish lives God's children are living—making use of the merits of Calvary for their own salvation only, and living for themselves. Sacrifice is counted a foolish thing by the followers of the crucified Christ! In the day of eternity, how few will bear the marks of the Lamb! How short the time to suffer and to sacrifice in the service of souls, how paltry will things look at the Judgment of Christ! How *mean* we shall feel, when we see in the light of the eyes of fire how little we have given our lives in the service of a world lying in the evil one.
>
> How we bless God, my husband and I, for the opportunity, in the little while, of counting all loss for Christ. We feel how little it is, how brief

> the time! We covet that our God may do the most with us in our short lives—and then we shall be together to rejoice over the glorious harvest for all eternity. Think you that we shall regret *any* sacrifice then? When we look in our beloved Master's face, shall we regret giving our home and our lives for Him? Oh the joy now! What will it be then?

The first country she visited was Sweden, and her account of an incident which took place on the journey gives us a glimpse of her single-minded longing to bear witness under any and every circumstance, and her quiet confidence that God, who was sending her, would keep her all the way.

> After writing on the train yesterday, heard some singing of Swedish hymns in the third-class carriage. I went out into the corridor and opened the door between. I saw a large number of men with their hymn books open, singing away! Some of the passengers in our carriage followed me, and one young man said something to me. I touched my lips and shook my head. Then he fetched out a Bible. I went for mine, and showed it to him. Finally it occurred to me that we might talk in that way! I took his Bible and found Galatians 2:20, and he read it, looking at me so brightly. Then I turned to Romans 6:11, "Reckon ye yourselves to be dead indeed unto sin." He replied, "Ja! Ja!" I turned on to Acts 19. "Have ye received the Holy Ghost since ye believed?" Then to Acts 1:8, "Ye shall

> receive power" and Acts 2:39, "The promise is unto *you*!" He followed intelligently, then looked upward and said, "Ja!" Someone else knew a little English and took my Bible, saying, "You a believer?" It was so good, this fellowship through the medium of the Word of Life.
>
> I reached Stockholm at 9:50 p.m., after fourteen hours in the train, but no more tired than after a much shorter journey at home. The Lord had carried all the way. Truly He is "El Shaddai"—the "God who is enough."
>
> "When I sent you . . . lacked ye anything? And they said, *nothing*" (Luke 22:35).

The first time it becomes necessary to speak through an interpreter is a testing experience; and Mrs. Penn-Lewis commented on her fears and how God undertook for her.

> Today I have had two meetings. The first in a private drawing-room, with about forty Christians present. It was with much "fear and trembling" (1 Cor. 2:3) that I went. The adversary kept telling me that it was impossible to "grip" the meeting by interpretation. Waiting upon the Lord to be shown *how* to speak through the interpreter, the light dawned on me. I saw that I was to do exactly as I would in England, with my interpreter as a kind of "echo" by my side. I was to ignore him and speak directly to the people.

> As I rose to speak, with the first word I knew that God was there. It was perfect liberty, and as easy as if I had been speaking to English folk. I soon forgot my "echo," and so did everyone else. God took hold of every heart. After silent prayer, I rose thinking that the meeting was over, but nobody moved. There seemed a deep hush, and the awe of God's presence upon all. I asked if they had any questions, and answered those that were asked. Then I asked all who meant to have God's best to answer "Yes," and a "Ja!" came. Still no one moved. Then we went to prayer again, and souls poured out their hearts to God in their own language. Then—after a two-hour meeting—we broke up.
>
> This, for a first gathering, showed prepared ground. God is evidently going to move among us. The relief to my own soul that interpretation, in God's hand, was not going to prove a fetter was immense.

An account of the final meeting of this first series of gatherings in a foreign country is worth including, showing the way in which the speaker was set to one side and the Spirit of God Himself did the work.

> On the last day in the afternoon, I spoke again on the New Life in Christ, dealing yet further with practical difficulties discovered in personal dealing during the interval for lunch. At the close we asked any to leave who wished to

do so, as we were going to spend a little time in waiting upon God, specially with the thought of the "enduement of power." I confess, I only expected a few to stay, but only five or six went out, and there were about 300 people purposed to wait upon God without hurry. It seemed incredible, but upon our knees we went! I may add here that in Sweden it is not the custom to kneel, but to sit and bow the head. That day, however, they instinctively turned to their knees.

I said that anyone might pray, if they would be brief and definite, as we were short of time. A few led in prayer, but so softly that not many could hear, and the noise of the traffic outside made it more difficult. I then rose and said that no one need attempt to listen—that the impossibility of hearing one another tended all the more to our isolation with God. It did not matter if several prayed together; let everyone deal with God direct, as if they were really alone.

A moment's pause, and then almost the whole meeting broke out into audible prayer, each dealing with God for their own personal needs. For about ten minutes the murmur of prayer rose and fell, like the rippling of a brook; a hush, and then prayer again and again, from all parts of the Hall. Men's voices, and women's, then a pastor. I stood and looked on amazed.

> There was no jar, only beautiful harmony, yet everyone praying in his own language (there were some Finns and Norwegians there also), in complete oblivion of the presence of others. I could only think of that wondrous day when "all began to speak as the Spirit gave them utterance."
>
> We rose from our knees, many with streaming eyes and the holy awe upon us, as we sat awhile in instinctive silence which told of the direct presence of God.

This visit to Sweden was followed by one to Russia in the following year—1897—from mid-January through mid-February. She traveled by train through Berlin and Warsaw to St. Petersburg and, later on, to Moscow. At that time there was a movement of the Spirit among the aristocratic and wealthy families of that country, and much of her work lay in these circles. One comment from one of the Russian Christians reveals both the need that was there and the equipment that God gave to the messenger He had chosen to send.

> Twenty years have we waited for you! God sent a messenger twenty years ago to tell us of *Christ for us*, and one or two others come now and then with the same message; but now God has sent another revelation: *Christ in you*. Twenty years have we been babes, but now it shall be *no more*! We are so, so happy!

Mrs. Penn-Lewis' witness to the power of a Spirit-filled life resulted in God Himself coming into His own in heart after heart. But she had time also for those in the very early days of seeking the Saviour, and a love for the unconverted that never failed through the years. One incident she herself recorded highlights this aspect of her life.

> A young student—a Jew, Israel V_____ by name—came to see me. A lady sat by me and translated our conversation. He did not waste any time. He said last year he had been given a New Testament and, on reading it, God showed him Jesus Christ as the Messiah; and now he knew God was working in him—he knew he could *see* the Kingdom; but what did it mean to *enter* the Kingdom? (and he read the two verses in John 3). Had he to hear a *voice*? I said the Holy Spirit came sometimes like a soft and gentle wind, and you *heard nothing*—He had come thus to him.
>
> He continued, that he was conscious of inward battle and how sometimes "Israel V_____ had his way!" But he wanted to know God so that others might *know* that he knew Him, for so few people seemed really to know Him, and he wanted to be used by God the very most that was possible. God gave me answers from the Bible and made everything clear to him. He was so intelligent and so receptive. He got assurance that he was in the Kingdom that night.

Two weeks in St. Petersburg packed with meetings and interviews took a heavy toll on her all-too-meager supply of physical strength, and her friends persuaded her to take a brief break in Moscow for a change of air and rest, traveling with a young lady who would look after her. There something occurred that shows the simplicity of her trust in the Saviour, whose commission she was fulfilling. She shall tell the story in her own words.

> Last night I developed a cold in my head, which became very severe. Mr. S_____ called in the evening, and seemed much alarmed about it. He evidently thought I was going to have influenza—so I agreed to stay in bed today. It certainly got bad very quickly. My eyes were running like a tap and my face became raw with the water.
>
> Mr. S_____ came again on the Saturday afternoon, and I seemed very little better. A cough was coming, and I saw that the Lord would have to work for me or I should be laid up. Mr. S_____ began to talk about a doctor, so I thought he considered me pretty well gripped by the cold.
>
> My companion went out with him to get some things, and I took the chance to talk to the Lord about it. I saw the Lord's dealings with me. In the heart of Russia—practically alone, with a bad cold getting a grip on me; with no single

> soul to ask to pray with me—and in a hotel far away from even the friends I had in Russia. A telegram to Petersburg would take half a day at least, for things move slowly here. It was a blessed test. No shade of fear or question. I was *not alone*! It was all the same in the heart of Russia as in England. How lovely to be put into fresh places to prove His power! I just knelt and told the Lord that the work *had* to be finished, and I must be well, and that He could not let the friends be disappointed. Then I opened my Bible at "Jesus, knowing the power proceeding from Him had gone forth, said . . . Thou art healed of thy plague." *And it was done!*
>
> The running water of eyes and nose stopped instantly. My companion came in; she looked at me: "You are better?" "Yes," I said, "the Lord has done it." I then was fresh and bright for writing, and had a good night.
>
> On Sunday afternoon Mr. S_____ came for me and was very astonished.

The program Mrs. Penn-Lewis undertook at this time is one that many enjoying full health and strength might well have recoiled from. After Russia in January and February, her engagements in 1897 included conferences and meetings in Norwich, Derby, Manchester, London, Glasgow, Dunfermline, Edinburgh and Birmingham. Then a brief period at home, given largely to writing, after which came visits to Doncaster, Brighton,

Richmond and Finsbury. She spent August in Switzerland, then was on the move again to Swansea, Langland Bay, Rothesay, Manchester again, four days of meetings in Leicester, and the Annual Meetings of the South Africa General Mission (now the Africa Evangelical Fellowship) in London. Then to Coventry, Edinburgh, Belfast, and in December meetings at the headquarters of the Church Army in London. The odd times between these various commitments were occupied with writing, dealing with a growing correspondence, interviews, and local meetings in Leicester.

In 1898 she was abroad again—Russia, Finland, and Denmark in the spring; then return visits to Finland and Denmark in June. One result of these visits was the production of many of the booklets which had followed the issue of *The Pathway to Life in God.*

This time in Russia there was opposition to Mrs. Penn-Lewis' visit on the ground that so many "sectarians," as they were called, had attended her meetings held the year before. The attention of the ecclesiastical authorities had been drawn to this; and as fines, confiscations, imprisonment and exile were remorselessly imposed upon any who dared to differ from the Czar's religion, the meetings had almost entirely to be of a strictly private character and by invitation only. It was not until 1905 that an edict of liberty of conscience in matters of religion was declared.

It is interesting to see how writing was continually born out of ministry. Mrs. Penn-Lewis always declared that she was no authoress, but only put on paper the things the Spirit of God was showing her so that she could pass them on to others. A book originally entitled *Conflict in the Heavenlies* was, for instance, the sub stance of some messages given on Good Friday of 1897 in the China Inland Mission hall. After running through two editions, it was enlarged and finally published under its present title, *The Warfare with Satan and the Way of Victory.*

After all, it is like the Lord, who commanded the remains left over after the feeding of the five thousand to be gathered up, to preserve for future generations light which He Himself had given.

The year 1898 saw the issue of another book, *The Message of the Cross*; which in 1903—as fresh understanding had been given her on this great central theme of the Christian message—was rewritten and given its present title, *The Cross of Calvary and its Message.* So that we may catch a glimpse of something of what this book cost her, we will once again let her speak for herself.

> Good Friday was blessed! God never gave me such a message before—the whole day on Calvary. And He took me to "Calvary" in experience for a fortnight before, from the hour the message began to open to me.... All this winter it has been, again and again, a being "delivered

unto death for Jesus' sake"; and the ten days preceding the Good Friday meetings [at Mildmay] were the most awful ten days of all my spiritual history.

God gave me "the word of the cross" on March 28th, and from that moment it seemed as if all hell was roused. His hand was upon me, writing all He showed me, and I wrote in the teeth of it for a week. . . . I thought I had seen His death before, but it was from the *outside*—the Judgment Hall, the forsaking, etc.—but now it was from the *inside* of His heart. It was a drinking of "His cup" I had never known before, and in the darkest hour He gave me Psalm 22. . . .

I felt the anguish to Him of that moment when all the devils of hell seemed mocking, in the voices of those who stood round the cross, that His trust in God had been fruitless—that God would have answered *if* He had been pleased with Him, *and His God had failed Him!*

My heart was at rest, if it was His pathway. And then there came to me His definite promise, that the message of Calvary so deeply wrought in the experience of the cross should go forth to the very ends of the earth and carry with it the power of the cross and "life out of death" to seeking souls. . . .

If the real sight of the cross will come to others as it did to me, it will indeed be a blessed book.

> It is very sacred to me. It seems as if my very life is in it, baptized in the valley of weeping. It is more "of God" than anything I have written, and seems the outcome of six years of His deep work in me. As though all had culminated in this! But it is "always delivered unto death." The book will always be stamped with Calvary to me.

This book is indeed a classic on the Atonement in all its aspects, and has been translated into a number of languages. It seems right, therefore, that two comments made on it at the time should be included here. "An old doctrine in a new light" was the heading of a hearty commendation of the book by Rev. Griffith Ellis in a Welsh magazine. Oswald Chambers, writing a personal letter from Dunoon College, Scotland, says:

> Your *Cross of Calvary* is preeminently of God. The splendid treasure of pain, your pain, has merged into the greatness of God's power. Your book reaches clearly and grandly what the Spirit witnesses to in the Bible and in our hearts, viz: that "the Way of God" flatly contradicts common sense, and by utmost despair the Holy Ghost leads to resurrection triumph.
>
> *The breakdown of the natural virtues* seems to be the point at which most regenerated lives are cast into despair. Your book will help those to understand that this despair must end in death to natural goodness and self, and be raised by

the power of God into inconceivably glorious power and peace and liberty of life. . . .

You are clearer and clearer each time you write, and each day you grow from those past days of mysterious crucifixion, which is an open secret to those of us who have the witness of the Spirit.

CHAPTER 5

THE CENTRAL CROSS

THERE are few engaged in any kind of Christian ministry who would not admit in theory that the Christian message is centered in the cross of Christ; but there are many who in their hearts would ask the question that at one time presented itself with considerable force to Mrs. Penn-Lewis: "How can I *always* preach the cross?" This question was partially solved for her when on one occasion she was visiting Edinburgh and staying with Rev. and Mrs. W.D. Moffat. Years later, after Mr. Moffat's homecall, she wrote:

> To Mr. Moffat I owe, under God, the first understanding of the trust committed to me in the message of the cross in its deeper aspect to the Christian. . . . With only glimmering light, I once said to him, "How can I *always* preach the cross, for there are only so many verses about it, and I cannot use them again and again?" But

> he kept me up that night till the early hours of the morning, explaining, urging, pleading, that I would not be diverted from the message God had illuminated to me.
>
> I went away from that Edinburgh visit to some meetings for Christians at Gordon Hall, Liverpool, asking God to show me the way never to give an address on any theme without "preaching the cross," and to my astonishment in those days, as I was speaking on many themes concerning the Christian life, I found myself, in the heart of the message, showing the cross as the center of every theme. Then I saw that all aspects of the spiritual life could be shown to have, as their basis, Calvary; and that *all spiritual truth radiated from the cross.*

Cannot you and I learn something from this? There is so much that would be termed "evangelical ministry" which supplies much useful information drawn from the Bible, but the saving power of God is not manifest, because the cross is not being presented to both sinner and saint in the power of the Spirit as the one meeting place with God at any time or stage of life. The place of deliverance from the dominion of sin, self and Satan is at the cross of Christ and nowhere else. The Spirit of God will set His seal on no other message. The Living Christ can only be known by this gateway which leads to Him.

But let us step back now to the early months of 1898. Her second journey to Russia—again in January—proved to be the occasion for another lesson that Mrs. Penn-Lewis needed to learn again and again. She tasted something of the spiritual conflict behind what was outwardly useful work. Writing to Miss Soltau, she expressed her experience in these terms:

> That last week the pressure on my spirit grew, until I was spent. . . . "Pressed down exceedingly, insomuch as we despaired even of life—but we had the answer [that it was] death in ourselves, that we might not trust [have any resource] in ourselves, but in God who raiseth the dead" (see 2 Cor. 1:8–9).
>
> I saw that it needed His Risen Life *now* to raise me from the depths to the place of victory, far above all principality and power, and that thus the travail would be over, the ground wrenched from the foe, and the atmosphere clear. I rose up, and the life returned. On that Wednesday night the people were broken, on the Thursday it was *glory*, and throughout those last days God swept in in mighty power.
>
> Then I understood that, clothed in the "armor of light," God sends us to the dark places of the earth to set our foot down and *take the victory* in the name of the Lord. That in the travail we may be "pressed down" until we are "as good as dead," in order that the resurrection life of Jesus may lift us up in triumph to the place of victory, "far above all." Then the hosts of darkness are

> defeated and the Spirit of Life can work unhindered in the souls around us. Blessed be God!

She was no more immune from times of depression than you and I are. The time in Russia had taken much out of her physically, and as soon as she relaxed the full force of her tiredness weighed her down. She finally felt that she had unconsciously been living on her old natural life again, and for this reason the old symptoms—exhaustion, cough, etc.—were being manifested. Then, to use her own words, she says: "There and then I definitely dropped my body at the cross as never before. . . . Since then, blessed be God, I am quite well." A visit to Nottingham for meetings seemed to be a time of recommissioning and encouragement; so much so that in May she was once again on her way overseas for a second visit to Denmark, and then on to Sweden and Finland.

The pattern of blessing in Denmark was of the same kind as that seen in Russia. She had some contacts with those who were using her booklets, particularly *The Pathway to Life in God* and *The Glorious Secret,* and in between the time spent in traveling and a full program of meetings, hours were spent in personal conversations. One extract from her diary gives a picture of the ministry to individuals, or the few, for which she always found time.

> At 11 a.m. my group arrived, and we sat around the table, about twelve of us. One, a lady I had not seen in February, said, "You have come this

time *for me!*" She had heard nothing about conformity to the death of Jesus, but all the winter she had been passing through it and others had said she was backsliding. She could not think what it meant, only she had the assurance herself that she was in the hand of God. Then came *The Pathway to Life in God* and she saw what God was doing. She is at the head of a large work, and is manifestly a surrendered soul.

All this group *meant* to deal with God, so without reserve we traced the story of the Jordan crisis and the opened heavens which finally led to the real Calvary, the grave, the resurrection, and the Throne. We sat over this for two hours, and it was a most precious time. Three months ago they were not ready for it, but God had laid hold of some then and had opened still more to them since, through the printed messages. . . . He had indeed prepared them, and now the Lord has an inner group going on with Him to become buried corns of wheat in fruitfulness for Denmark.

At one o'clock they hurried away, and at 3 we had the afternoon meeting, a much longer one, and such a deep hush and receptivity. God is evidently going to deepen and deepen His work. The meeting over, they gave me tea and sent me off for a drive, and at 8 p.m. we had our fourth drawing-room meeting. Most blessed indeed: The attention never flagged as I spoke

> for nearly an hour and a half. . . . We did not leave until 11 o'clock.

In Sweden the work was also full of lasting value. A glimpse of the final meeting of this part of the tour gives us very simply an idea of what God was doing.

> The last meeting was the best of all! To watch the deeper and deeper breaking, the clearer and clearer light on the faces, tells one much. God had given them the Holy Spirit, and now He was just showing them how the Spirit would lead them into the path of the cross. How He would reveal to them the Life of Jesus; how death with Him must needs be for fruitfulness. It has been so clear, and His presence so manifest; one could see how it met the souls.
>
> The booklets I had with Irie, hoping to reserve some for Finland, were all taken at the first meeting, and with joy some of the older workers said, "This is what Sweden needs—we have been waiting for the message of the cross."

And so, to Finland in June! One of the first contacts pinpointed an interesting and important aspect of personal work, and it is recorded in full.

> The teacher of English at the University of Helsinki called to see me. He had written for permission to translate all my printed messages into Swedish [then the dominant language of the country], so had come at once to see me.

He was truly being taught of God. Converted in America many years ago, God had been leading him deeply. He knew he had the *light* of all that it meant to be crucified with Christ, but not the *life*. . . .

Telling me of his conversion, he said a very true thing—a fact that has come to me many times, yet I never heard it said before. He told me that God had awakened him on board ship, and in America led him to an evangelist who preached Christ to him, and his heart drank it in. Then the devil interfered, for the evangelist had said, "Now *you must believe*"; his attention was turned to *his* part, *believing*, and he said, "How can I believe?"—and fell into years of darkness and real unbelief. His heart had received the gospel and he was already believing until he was told *he* must believe! Ten years or more passed, struggling to believe, instead of looking to the finished work of Christ. It has occurred to me that, in dealing with souls, as soon as you turn their attention to *their act of faith*, there is a cloud and a feeling that they cannot.

So also with God's children. Absorbed with the finished work of Christ, dwelling upon it, the heart *believes* without knowing it. This is God's marvelous plan of drawing the soul out of itself and its sins by giving it a Saviour on Calvary—a center of attention outside itself. Then He enters and does the work within.

This last sentence is very true. When a life is committed into the hand of God, He undertakes to work in every part of the life. So it was with Mrs. Penn-Lewis: He permitted her after her return from this trip to prove His power to lead and teach in very different circumstances.

In December a serious breakdown in her health made a complete stoppage of all public work necessary. She was able to accept this as from Him, and to set herself to wait upon Him and to seek to see something of what the future held for her. The first five weeks of 1899 were spent at Eastbourne in the care of friends, and slowly a measure of restoration was given. A "Prayer Letter" dated February 20th, 1899, allows us to see something of her attitude of heart at this time. She wrote:

> I have no words to tell you the thanksgiving that fills my heart as I look back over the Lord's wondrous dealings in 1898. . . . It was a year of fellowship with His sufferings—purely from a spiritual standpoint—that no words can express, to teach me in deep reality the message of His cross. It was His own hand that led me, and His own voice that cheered me through the deep waters, in the conflict with the powers of darkness. . . .
>
> For months I have had God's messages in writing, and through pressure of correspondence and innumerable small matters claiming

> ceaseless attention they have never gone to print. I have endeavored to keep the correspondence in check, sometimes writing late at night, but even with the help of a secretary it has been impossible. My heart had been grieved over the unfinished booklets.
>
> Then came God's withdrawal of power to go on, and the imperative necessity of rest. This was my release. . . . He showed me that if I was to write what He gave me, I must be entirely withdrawn aside with Him, even as Moses in the Mount with God, and let the business of the camp alone.

A letter from Baron Nicolay of Finland to Mr. Penn-Lewis quaintly puts the matter in another way.

> I am sorry to hear of your dear wife's illness. May she consider that the earthen vessel is not a "heavenly vessel" in this sense: that a poor earthen vessel does need careful handling, not to break before the time. It is a favorite dodge of Satan, if he cannot keep us below the mark to push us beyond the mark, and make our activity consume us. . . . Maybe St. Paul had, for the same reason, to be put in prison for two years. We should have grieved over the "lost time," but certainly it was not lost in God's sight, who ordained it so.

On February 22nd, restored to something of her usual health, Mrs. Penn Lewis crossed once more to St. Petersburg, this time for rest and quiet, away from the constant calls which seemed unavoidable in England.

No meetings were taken during this visit, but the only relaxation from close writing was the daily carriage drive in the keen, bracing air.

Then just before Easter, when apparently quite well, she was suddenly struck down with a sharp attack of pleurisy. That afternoon she had driven out in 17 degrees of frost, and the keen air aroused a dormant inflammation in her delicate lungs. With little or no reserve strength, she rapidly sank to the lowest ebb of life. Four Russian women of God, ladies of "honorable estate," prayed faithfully to God for her. For more than three weeks the fight of faith never relaxed, but after an assurance given, on Easter Eve, to those caring for her, the patient began to regain strength.

"I have no fear about the issue of my illness," reads a letter to Mr. Penn-Lewis written on April 26th. "My work is not yet done!" It continues:

> God is in it, and He is only equipping for better service by and by. The first week was the worst. . . . One night I felt myself becoming unconscious; it seemed as if my spirit was slipping away, when with such a "pulling together" I said, "*I will not die!*" and then I came back to consciousness. God is bringing me into deeper and deeper rest. It would be much easier, to the flesh, to be suddenly healed! But I see that I

> must leave absolutely all question as to time—otherwise there is no surrender. . . . It will not go one point beyond His limit, and He will do His work in the very best way.

On May 3rd, after six weeks in bed, her temperature was normal for the first time, and immediately berths were booked for the journey home a fortnight later, in faith that the Lord would continue to answer the prayers of His children. The tide had turned.

For some time before this she had been engaged in writing a book of exposition dealing with the Song of Solomon, *Thy Hidden Ones,* and soon after her recovery she found that her power to write had returned. "Today and henceforth," runs an entry in her diary, as she took up this task again, "my keynote will be *leaning upon the Beloved* as never before." It is not an intellectual treatise, but was born out of God's dealings with her *deep down within.* She herself put it in this way: "So it was with *Thy Hidden Ones,* and other books and articles—always from the center." Later that year her publishers, Messrs. Marshall Brothers, told her that this book was selling faster than any of the others. It is still being sold and, years later, brings help to many.

By July Mrs. Penn-Lewis was able to attend the Keswick Convention. Year after year she had been present at the convention; and knowing the tide of blessing which God gave through her proclamation of His Word, many were the voices urging that she should speak at the public gatherings, but hitherto the Lord had not so led. Now, in 1899, for the first time she became one of the speakers at the ladies' meetings, by invitation of the Trustees, and very tender was the welcome she received from many old friends on this, her first public appearance since God had so marvelously raised her up from the edge of death.

She spoke with genuine authority, not only opening up the Scriptures but applying them to home relationships and showing the way into a life that in itself was a witness to God's grace and power. As was so often the case in after years, it was not until she stood up to speak that she was lifted above her physical weakness.

After Keswick, she once more retired from the well-received public work and went abroad, for she felt that the Lord would have her take her rest as solemnly and faithfully as her service. "I saw then," she wrote, "that to maintain a deep stream from God in public work, the messenger needed to watch as keenly for the voice of God crying '*Halt!*' as for the word 'Go forward.' I learned again that to follow the Spirit of God, and be blind and deaf to the voice of man, meant being led into richer and fuller service than before."

One happy summer month was therefore spent with her husband in the Channel Islands, and the autumn in Switzerland with her Russian friends. Afterwards she joined Mr. Penn-Lewis at Eastbourne for the Christmas season.

In the following summer, 1900, came a call to visit Canada and the United States, and immediately after Keswick, Mr. and Mrs. Penn-Lewis sailed for Canada, spending the August vacation together there. They especially enjoyed the grandeur of Niagara Falls. At the end of the month, Mr. Penn-Lewis sailed back to England, but she remained behind on the service of the King until the end of October. After some fruitful meetings in Ottawa, Kingston and Toronto, she traveled on to the United States.

The first piece of work for Mrs. Penn Lewis was the conducting of four "Quiet Days" in a country house some five miles from Peekskill-on-Hudson, N.Y., the home of Mrs. C. de Peyster Field, at whose invitation the visit to this country had been undertaken. Thirty guests were accommodated in the house, and a stage coach came up daily from Peekskill bringing others, so that there were fifty present for dinner each day. The days were very full, beginning with morning prayers at 7:45, and meetings during the day were interspersed with many interviews with souls seeking personal help. The Lord was present in manifest power, and a deep, intensive work was done in the lives of the Christian workers there gathered, so that when the last day came there was not one guest but had really been met with by the Lord in a very vital way. Mrs. Penn Lewis wrote:

> I have seen God deal with some souls out of a group, but never before with every soul present.

> We shall none of us ever forget it. Yet during the two days *preceding*, I had one of the keenest conflicts I have ever known—I almost fled!
>
> > "Though hot the fight why quit the field?
> > Why should I either fly or yield,
> > Since Jesus is my mighty Shield?"
>
> These words just brought me through, and then the Lord broke forth upon us with visions of God! During the four days I had practically four meetings each day, and was carried beautifully through.

After a brief rest, she traveled on by train to Chicago, arriving on September 24th in time for the closing meetings of a ten-days "Workers Conference" at the Moody Bible Institute, in which she was to take part. The first evening—as she, unseen, stepped into the meeting hall to see the working of it—she heard herself being spoken of by Dr. R.A. Torrey, the President, "in a very American way" as "one of the most gifted speakers the world has known"—which embarrassed her greatly.

This conference was followed by some special meetings in the lecture hall of the Institute, under her entire charge. For five packed days she spoke to different groups. In addition, she met privately with numerous individual Christian workers, some of whom had come from afar to consult with her. All this was on top of the several meetings each day. These were crammed, with people standing in the doorways and along the passages, as she followed the Lord's leading to "dig deep." It was a most blessed time.

Then by train she went back East to Northfield, Massachusetts, the birthplace of Dwight L. Moody and the site of his other school for Christian workers—where she spoke twice at chapel. One little incident during that two-day visit shows the attitude of respect and affection with which she regarded those whom it had pleased God to call and use in His service. She said, "Of course I visited *Round Top*, and as I sat on a seat near Mr. Moody's grave, I thought of the wondrous honor accorded to him in his earthly record—that of being a true winner of souls—and of the glory of his coronation day."

After a few days' rest back at Peekskill, she then went to New York City and was invited by Rev. A.B. Simpson to give a message at the convention being held in the Gospel Tabernacle there.

> The Lord gave me so keen a message on "how Saul lost his crown" that it made me almost sick to have to give it a stranger, and to strangers! But I obeyed, and God sealed the word. I lunched at their home, and returned to Hephzibah House quite exhausted with the severity of my message. Speaking again at the Gospel Tabernacle on the following Sunday afternoon, I heard that the severe message on Wednesday had done execution; some in real crises had been helped, and thanked me for my faithfulness.

This was followed by two days of meetings for workers at the Harlem Branch of the YWCA Then Rev. A.B. Simpson drove her to the Missionary Institute on Nyack Heights, where she spent two very full days with the students. Back again in New York City, she addressed a large meeting of women in the NYC YWCA auditorium, and then a group of forty deaconesses engaged in the parishes of various city churches. This was followed by a two-day sojourn in Philadelphia, where she had a few meetings at the Reformed Episcopal Church of the Atonement pastored by Dr. D.M. Stearns. Then back to New York City, from which she sailed for home. An impression of her feelings about her visit to America is revealed in this extract from her diary.

> I left for England by the *Oceanic* on October 31st. The one-word ringing in my ears during the whole of my visit was *Foundations*. I was reminded that the wise builder "digged deep," and this briefly describes the need of the Christians in the United States, for crowds are easily drawn and quickly moved.
>
> *Deep subsoil work* is the one great need. May God equip His instruments in that land and all whom He sends forth to bear His messages there, making them wise master-builders—laying a good foundation, so that in the testing day when the floods come and break upon the buildings, they shall be found to have been "well builded" (Luke 6:48).

CHAPTER 6

REVIVAL AND THE AFTERMATH

THE years 1901 and 1902 were mainly spent in writing. *The Story of Job* was written during a protracted stay in Davos, Switzerland, under medical supervision, in hope of stopping the progress of the lung weakness which was yet obvious after her serious illness in Russia two years before. This book was written with the same liberty and divine unveiling as her message on the Song of Solomon and was so manifestly "gold out of the furnace" that a writer in *The Christian* spoke of it in this way:

> Mrs. Penn-Lewis . . . proves herself not merely to have intellectually and intelligently comprehended the book, but to have entered spiritually and experientially into its inmost thought, and to have passed through, in some degree, the sorrows of the patriarch. . . . From first to last, the terrible experience of the sufferer, and the restoration and the joy at last, are shown to be

> the dealings of the only wise God our Saviour with His child, whom in love and faithfulness He afflicted and exalted. These illuminative pages contain not so much a study as a meditation. Though full of thought and of Christian experience, they come from, and appeal to, the heart rather than the intellect, and yet there is more enlightened and enlightening intellectual discernment than in many commentaries.

This was followed by the little book *Face to Face*, an exquisite "cameo" meditation on the inner life of Moses, with whom God spoke "face to face." It had been written in the space of one week at Eastbourne in May 1900, at the request of Messrs. Marshall Brothers, to form one of their "Quiet Hour" series. Two thousand copies of this book were sold in the first four months, and it was the means of making the other writings of Mrs. Penn-Lewis much more widely known. Up to this time all had been issued privately, without advertisement, and chiefly circulated among those who had heard the writer speak at conventions and other gatherings. The publication of this book through ordinary business channels, and the prominence given to it in the advertisement columns of *The Life of Faith*, led to larger sales and more readers in many lands.

When once again it was possible for Mrs. Penn-Lewis to throw herself into active ministry, it was perhaps fitting that she should find herself drawn into the prayerful planning which was going on, at first at the instigation of two ministers, for a Keswick Convention to be held in her native Wales. She was wholehearted in anything into which she felt that God was leading her, and was largely instrumental in formulating step-by-step the original plans. So it was that the Llandrindod Convention came into being. From the very first meetings held, the blessing of God was seen. At the first convention the attendance by ministers was such that a well-known missioner's involuntary remark was: "Wales may be the cradle of the evangelists for the coming revival."

Towards the end of 1902 she received an invitation to go to India, which after a good deal of prayer and consideration was accepted. March 1903, then, saw her in India. The fact that *The Pathway to Life in God* and others of her booklets had already preceded her meant that there were many who sought her counsel. There were some earnest folk who tended to hold the truth stated in Romans 6 and Galatians 2:20 as a "line of teaching," grasping it in the natural mind and making a system of it. This meant the employment of language which went "beyond that which is written," and was causing strife. If there is a possibility of "knowing Christ after the flesh," is always possible that the very truth of God may be taken hold of by the flesh and the fleshly mind and preached in "the wisdom of man"—and made powerless. Perhaps Mrs. Penn Lewis' summary of her attitude to all this will be best seen through a letter she wrote at the time to one of those involved.

I have seen the work at _____ and met all the souls concerned, and I see how the human presentation of the blessed Calvary deliverance has blurred the message and thrown many off the track.

I feel most deeply that the "experiential" side has hidden the power of the Divine side, and prevented the Holy Spirit from showing the work of Christ alone as the basis of faith. In every soul I have dealt with I have seen the disastrous confusion and despair produced by preaching an experience instead of the work of Christ. I can only cry to God to enable you to lift up CHRIST, instead of a dead self.

I have taken every soul I have dealt with to the Lord, and sifted before Him all the fruits of [your teaching] in these confused ones; gone over the Scripture concerned, and watched and prayed to see where the error is; and clearer and clearer God has shown me it is the danger of preaching an experience instead of Christ. Of preaching a "death" that is not the application of Christ's death by the Holy Ghost but an experimental "death" beyond that which is written.

"I fear lest . . . as the serpent beguiled Eve by his subtlety, so your minds should be corrupted from the simplicity that is in Christ." It is the mind, not the heart, that is the trouble. The mind beguiled from the simplicity of Christ.

> Your experience may easily be of God and yet the mind not able to interpret it clearly. . . .
>
> Dear friend, it is with deep yearning and many tears that I am jealous with a jealousy of God concerning you. It is a solemn thing to hinder Christ from reaching His own, however unconscious we may be of it. It is heartbreaking to see you frustrating the very longing of your own heart to help God's servants. . . Surely He can illuminate your mind and heart, to give you a deeper sympathy *and* love in dealing with souls.
>
> How terrible it is to appear hard when your heart is full of love! How terrible to put iron chains of bondage on others—souls whom God has made free! "Where the Spirit of the Lord is, there is liberty."
>
> But God will bring you through into a large place, where your vision will be of God and you will carry to all around you the vision of God that brings self to the dust, and does not occupy the souls with their own miserable selves. Then souls will be drawn to the glorious Christ within you, and never see the earthen vessel at all. That is His way—and souls then know that they have met with Him.

And to a leading missionary in South India she wrote:

> It could hardly be possible for me to be here without hearing of the painful divisions of last

year. I think you know that for eight years my own service has been entirely at conventions and among Christian workers, and I have had to deal with every phase of the experiences and expressions along the line of Romans 6. This long time of continual service in many countries, among the most deeply taught of the servants of God, has made one acute to see at once where the line of expression is off the fine balance of the written Word, and to discern where the Holy Spirit does not bear witness. Where we are perfectly in line with the Scripture, rightly dividing the Word of Truth, the Holy Ghost commends the message to every man's conscience as coming from Him. What is from God, God seals with His Spirit. Is it not so?

Alas for the souls in despair and confusion, looking for an experience of "death" instead of resting on the work of Christ, which brings glad freedom and the positive inflowing of life from the Risen One.

And then this question of separation. It is my deep conviction that separation, as God wants it, can only be truly brought about by the Lord Himself, as the inevitable outcome of His manifested Presence. It has been sad to see souls thrown back from the fuller knowledge of God through *tennis* being emphasized as "unlawful," instead of the glorious Lord being lifted up, who will make His will known to every surrendered

> heart. May the Lord keep us from touching other lives by dealing with exterior things instead of preaching the fullness of Christ. . . .
>
> *Christ alone is the answer to each need.* If we could only unveil HIM, it would not be long before the souls would cry "Woe is me," and not need to be told of separation. God forgive us for emphasizing the negative instead of Him who is all in all, and is the drawing power unto Himself.

One of the by-products of this trip was the production of the booklet of Bible verses entitled *The Word of the Cross.* As it turned out, it was through the work that grew up around this little booklet—so small that it qualifies as one of the weak things which God according to His own wonderful plan designs to use—that eventually *The Overcomer* magazine came to be published. God had already provided a mission press in Madras with a set of eight machines which had been used for advertising a patent medicine in the United States—these being a free gift from the inventor in Pennsylvania. They were capable of printing a tiny booklet of sixteen pages, measuring two inches by three, at the rate of 100,000 per day, or 28 million per year. This mission press was in the charge of Dr. A.W. Rudisill, who had prayed for a long time, during which God was dealing with him in a special way, for suitable material for such a booklet. He was present at some of the meetings at which Mrs. Penn-Lewis spoke and became impressed with the thought that, since she had been raised up by God to spread the message of the cross, he should ask her to select verses bearing directly on this theme. She agreed to do this, and compiled it by devoting each page to some particular phase of uplifting the cross.

The booklet was issued from the M.E. Mission Press in Madras with none of the usual organization deemed necessary for the furthering of vast schemes; yet its circulation rapidly reached millions in Indian dialects alone. When the story became known, the Lord laid it upon the heart of a Jewish missionary in Jerusalem to prepare the booklet in Yiddish and Hebrew. Thus it came about, with no human forethought or plan, that almost the first translation issued from the Press was in the language of God's ancient people, in accordance with God's own principle "to the Jew first." Other translations poured in upon Dr. Rudisill from all lands. The British and Foreign Bible Society asked for 100,000 booklets in Tamil. The Salvation Army, and other Societies working in heathen lands, were not slow to see the value of the little printed messenger, and before very long the booklet was available in no less than one hundred languages and dialects.

Space forbids that we give details of the way in which God has worked through this tiny "missionary," but it is of interest to note that *The Word of the Cross* booklet was the first gospel message to enter Tibet. An army officer undertook to have a copy of the booklet in Spanish distributed to every Spanish-speaking household on the rock of Gibraltar. The demand for it throughout Great Britain was beyond all expectation, and the Lord laid it upon the late Mr. Thomas Hogben, Founder of the "One by One Band," to organize a systematic distribution throughout Britain and the Commonwealth, through the agency of the praying "Bands" associated with the "One by One" work.

One evangelist wrote of his use of the booklet:

> Hundreds have been won for Christ during the last three months, and scores of Christians have been led into the victorious life through its means. I asked one young man: "How long is it since God's Spirit spoke to you?" and he replied, "A young man gave me a Bible booklet. I read the first page, and then the second, where I read John 3:16, and since then I have had no rest. I know God can save me"—and He did.
>
> Seven young men came to my room, knowing nothing of the blessed life of victory—no holy boldness for the Lord, no passion for souls. We just got together and read the message in the booklet, then knelt silently before the Lord, until one after the other just sank prostrate before Him. We were there three hours, and since then each one of them has been marvelously changed. Hardly a week but they have

> been used of God to win souls. Two of these young men are going into the ministry. . . .
>
> At a free breakfast to the very lowest in a certain town, five remained behind to seek the Lord; and as I prayed that God would break them down, an ex-convict's wife said about the booklet's message, "That's the message to break them!" And it did. There was a desperate prisoner in the prison, and I asked the warden to let me see him. I went to the cell and got him on his knees, then read to him a few verses out of the booklet. It was the old message of Calvary, in all its power, and he was brought to Christ. . . .

It would be possible to multiply such testimonies to the value of the booklet; and it is still in print in a number of different languages. But it would be wrong to suggest that the same results are seen today. It is still being used, and has a special value as a means of opening up the message of the cross in Bible classes and home meetings. God has the right to use a booklet, a work, or a person as He wills; or if He so desires, to set them aside.

It *might* be that at a time for which we all long and pray—when the Holy Spirit is at work in power—this little book will *again* be picked up and bring a living presentation of the cross of Christ, and of His glory, to many hearts and lives.

We must now return from India to Wales. "All through 1903 and 1904 the underground currents were quickly deepening and sometimes breaking out to the surface, until the time drew near when the floodgates opened, and the Spirit of God broke out upon the land as a tidal wave, sweeping all before it." So ran Mrs. Penn-Lewis' comment on this particular period, a comment subsequently incorporated in the little book *The Awakening in Wales,* her account of the Welsh Revival.

Six Welsh ministers who had entered into the Spirit-filled life at the first Llandrindod Convention had agreed to meet once a month through the year for a quiet day with God. At the 1904 convention they held a midnight prayer meeting during which they consecrated themselves afresh to God for His use and definitely asked the Lord to raise up someone to usher in a revival. They returned to their respective churches burning with a new zeal and a new message, and in each place the flame of revival sprang up shortly after, resulting in a great ingathering of souls. Through them and their quickened people this revival spread from district to district, until it was said, "Wales is on fire."

In *The Life of Faith* for November 9th, 1904, there appeared a contribution from Mrs. Penn-Lewis in which, quoting a letter received from a well-known evangelist, she spoke of the "cloud the size of a man's hand" which had risen over Wales. Three weeks later she wrote: "We have prayed for revival. Let us give thanks! The 'cloud the size of a man's hand' about which the Rev. Seth Joshua wrote in October is now increasing. God is sweeping the southern hills and valleys of Wales with an old-time revival." From that time onward Mrs. Penn-Lewis became the chronicler of the revival, contributing a page to *The Life of Faith* each week, tracing the course of that movement of God, first throughout Wales and then through many lands and by many channels, reviving the sleeping Church of God and harvesting a great host of souls for His kingdom.

It was said by some, who perhaps only saw the emotional aspect of the work in Wales, that the Celtic temperament was the great factor in the whole movement, and particularly the Welsh singing! The Lord refuted this suggestion by manifesting the same melting power among Christians of different races and temperaments in India, China, Korea, Japan, and other missionary countries, and also in parts of Europe. A typical instance, in which Mrs. Penn-Lewis herself was the Lord's "channel," occurred in May 1905, at a conference for Christian workers in Germany. The Spirit of God came down in mighty power as His servant spoke of Calvary as the place of *unity* between Jew and Gentile (Eph. 2:11–18), that there can be no division *in* Christ, for Christ cannot be divided. The presence of God was intensely felt as a worker rose and said something in German. Then a brother rose and shook hands with another, with whom he had been at variance; then men and women from all parts of the gathering rose, confessing to one another hard thoughts and a spirit of division and disunity.

In the next meeting the message was on the power of Calvary's victory to deliver from the bondage of sin, the spirit of the world, the spirit of division, the power of the devil, and the life of self-pleasing; and the Lord did His own work among the 250 or so Christian workers gathered, not one soul remaining untouched.

At the close of the conference, the greater part of those present rose and pressed to the front to yield all to God and to receive the fullness of the Holy Spirit. Again was heard the chorus of prayer, as numbers prayed together without confusion, and on the following morning, for two hours, there was a stream of public testimony from old and young to what God had wrought in them.

Afterwards, Mrs. Penn-Lewis wrote in *The Life of Faith*:

> God *can* work, whatever the nationality or the temperament. In this conference we have seen that the melting was done by the Holy Spirit Himself, *through the Word of God*, with no persuasion or pleading, as there might have been had the messenger known the language of the people. Blessed be God for this evidence that the Holy Spirit can melt without the use of any means save the Word of God wielded by Himself, even in broken words translated into

> another tongue. . . . Undoubtedly what God has done this week will prepare the workers for revival, and we can only pray that all the surrendered ones may be as coals of fire scattered over the land.

For four years (November 1904 to the end of 1908) Mrs. Penn-Lewis continued to be a weekly contributor to *The Life of Faith*, first as recorder of the times of revival and afterwards with messages from the Word. In response to the expressed desire of Christian workers, many of these articles, giving a bird's-eye view of the movement of the Holy Spirit throughout the world, were reissued weekly on a separate sheet for wide distribution, under the general heading, "England, Awake!"

For some two years she also contributed articles to the pages of *The Christian*, which fulfilled an important service to the Church of God when, in 1908, they took the form of a series of articles on "An Hour of Peril."

In these Mrs. Penn-Lewis sought to place before the people of God a brief outline of the then-growing "Pentecostal Movement" based upon letters written by eyewitnesses in many parts of the world. The articles were not written in a spirit of opposition or adverse criticism, but with an earnest attempt to enable believers to discern for themselves certain points of danger, and with an urgent appeal to all to "try the spirits, whether they be of God," wherever supernatural manifestations were taking place.

The introductory article says:

> The tactics of Satan as an angel of light have been so subtle and his imitations of the working of the Holy Spirit so close, that however deep the inner conviction has been that false powers were at work in the Movement, the fear of touching anything that might be of God has checked the bold outspokenness which many faithful servants of God felt to be their duty. . . . Nevertheless, as fresh reports kept coming in from land after land where this movement was reaching, it was seen, almost without exception, that everywhere it brought division and separation among Christians. In some cases, unhappily, where there had been a true revival by the Spirit of God.

Dr. F.B. Meyer's comment on the articles was: "I think that the letters in *The Christian* are of high value just now. There is nothing else to guide these perplexed souls. What a strange thing it is! But surely the watchman should blow the trumpet and warn the people."

An extract from the book *The Warfare with Satan and the Way of Victory*, issued in 1906, when the Welsh Revival had already subsided, will show some thing of the spiritual background of the revival, and also some of the underlying causes of its cessation.

> If we look back at the history of the past decade, up to the time of the awakening in Wales, we can see how the Prince of Darkness was

working insidiously among the people, undermining their faith in the Scriptures as the Word of God, silencing the preaching of the cross to the utmost of his power, and drawing off great numbers into Theosophy . . . Christian Science . . . and spiritism.

At the same time, the Church was to a great extent powerless. Divisions, worldliness and carnal ease, on the whole marked her condition . . . until the Divine Spirit broke forth in Wales in Pentecostal power. The Church throughout the world was more or less awakened . . . and now all who know anything of the Spirit-filled life find themselves in a spiritual conflict with the hosts of wickedness in high places, and are discovering that every manifestation of the Holy Spirit is being met by a counterfeit of the evil one. In fact, the more "spiritual" a man is, the more open he is to the spirit-world—either good or evil powers. . . .

Let the believer seek an *experience* without the cross and all that it means in continuous crucifixion of *self*, and the evil one will give him all that he desires.

A clergyman's witness was: "In my case I found that any doubt, fear, agitation, want of love, self-exaltation—especially the feeling that God was going to do great things through me because I was so surrendered . . . brought false power and deception." The continuance of

> supernatural manifestations at first pure and of God, with a change of source unperceived by the ensnared believer, is the most subtle of the latest working of the enemy, and is the key to the strange and terrible inroad of spiritualistic manifestations among the most spiritual and surrendered souls in the Church of God.

Mrs. Penn-Lewis was now stressing the aspect of "war against the powers of darkness" more and more. The acceptance of the message of the cross in its fullness, as revealed in such passages as Romans 6 and Galatians 2:20, meant that we became "joined to the Lord" as "one spirit" (1 Cor. 6:17). Then the believer becomes conscious that his wrestling is not against flesh and blood, but against unseen spiritual foes "in the heavenlies." Such was her emphasis, leading to the view that the powers of darkness were pressing down upon the Church to keep her, if possible, from rising to her glorious place "far above all" in Christ. It was necessary, then, for every member of the body of Christ to understand the spiritual warfare so that they might triumph *in Christ* over Satan and his hosts as well as over sin and the world. It must be remembered that she had witnessed the devastation caused by false teaching concerning the Holy Spirit which followed so closely on the gradual dying down of the fires of revival in Wales. She described this disaster in these terms:

> In 1906 came what may be called "the hour and the power of darkness" upon the Church of

> Christ. . . . Lonely groups of believers who knew nothing of what was occurring in other parts of the world, and isolated workers unaware of the experiences of others, became conscious of the most extraordinary attempts of Satan to *imitate* the Holy Spirit in His workings.

A factor that had directed her thinking, and the development of her plans, was that Mr. Evan Roberts, through the strain brought about largely by eight months of daily, often almost continuous, meetings held in packed, ill-ventilated chapels, had completely broken down. Mr. and Mrs. Penn-Lewis then invited him to stay with them in their country home near Leicester, to rest and recuperate. His recovery was slow and intermittent; and during the long period of convalescence he began to tell his hostess of the many experiences of contact with supernatural forces he had gone through during the revival.

It was from this material, and in this way, that the book *War on the Saints* came to be written—a book with which Mrs. Penn Lewis' name has come to be specially associated in some quarters. It was finally published in 1912 after seven years work and has proven to be of great value to many who have had to deal with spirits and demon-possession, or in their own lives with deception and oppression by the powers of evil.

Once, when asked point blank by a young Christian: "Why cannot I get on with *War on the Saints*?" Mrs. Penn-Lewis rather surprisingly replied: "I hope you never will. It was written for those who have either been caught in the toils of overbalance caused by the deception of evil spirits or held in bondage by them. I trust that this will never be your experience, but that you may be enabled to live a healthy Christian life." One of the greatest contributions the book has made to a proper understanding of the Christian life is its very clear exposure of the perils of passivity. Unbiblical passivity, whether of the will, the mind; the conscience, or the spirit, is a condition which easily opens the believer to supernatural manifestations of the powers of darkness—violations of the human spirit which God is desiring to renew.

At this point events moved quickly. Ever since it had first been published, the demand for *The Word of the Cross* booklet was, as we have seen, phenomenal; so much so that a full-time secretary was now needed to attend to the business connected with it. A circular letter was sent out at intervals giving fuel for prayer to those interested in its distribution. In 1908 this was enlarged into a small, eight page bimonthly "occasional paper" with the title *The Word of the Cross*. The final issue for that year contained a note to the effect that it was now intended to increase the size of the paper to sixteen pages, and to record "not only the ever-increasing blessing attendant on the distribution of the booklet but messages of the preaching of the cross which may stir to renewed prayer and action all who have proved in their own lives the victory of Calvary."

Thus it was that in January of 1909, *The Overcomer* came into existence—both larger and as a monthly magazine. In January of 1910 a cover was added, increasing it to twenty pages, and in this format the magazine continued for the next five years.

CHAPTER 7

THE LATER YEARS

IT is more than probable that at this point there will be those among my readers who will feel that I am wrong even to suggest that Mrs. Penn-Lewis could ever be mistaken. It sometimes seems that the great figures in Christian ministry are regarded by many in rather the same way as ruling monarchs were in bygone days: "The King can do no wrong!" And yet this is a quite unscriptural attitude. Did not Peter, at one time so filled with the Spirit that as he walked down the street people were healed as his shadow fell on them, make a big mistake at Antioch? Were Paul and Barnabas infallible? If so, why did they quarrel about John Mark? Just because we are granted to know the fullness of the indwelling Holy Spirit, this does not guarantee us from all misconceptions and mistakes.

The feeling that one has been entrusted with some special ministry to the Church is not one that any of us can know much about, and it is something that is fraught with peculiar danger: It is possible, for instance, to get so absorbed in one particular aspect of truth that we get it out of perspective, to the great detriment of an all-round ministry, and then to develop a line of teaching causing separation from others of the Lord's people. Is it ever right to set yourself apart in this way? Can a witness to *God-given truth* ever become a cause of division among true children of God? These are questions calling for prayerful consideration.

Be all this as it may. It was at this point that Mrs. Penn-Lewis took the course of starting up her own conferences in which the warfare against the powers of darkness was to be the main thrust. She herself was always very careful to seek to lay the necessary foundation of our union with Christ in His death and resurrection, and sought definitely to maintain the balance of truth. But, as so often happens, her followers were not always so wise, and to this day the work has suffered from a stigma arising from the overbalance of those days.

The "Christian" world can be unkind. I have often been asked, for instance, if Mrs. Penn-Lewis was "quite normal" towards the close of her life. Such a judgment passed from lip to lip—probably based on the fact that some of those who termed themselves followers of "The Testimony" carried her teaching about warfare against the powers of darkness too far. Does this not commonly happen in the case of every spiritual teacher or leader?

In 1909 she withdrew from her sphere of service in the women's meetings at Keswick; and in 1911 she withdrew from the Council of the Llandrindod Convention. Her own version of these resignations was: "We parted, they 'giving me the right hand of fellowship'; that I should go to the saints with the warfare message, and *they* to the saints who needed other aspects of the truth."

It may help us to see all this in perspective if we give careful attention to what she herself wrote in announcing the first of her "Matlock Conferences," held in 1912.

> Large numbers of Christians attend conventions for the purpose of earnestly seeking a victorious life, but for lack of *personal application of the truths proclaimed to their individual difficulties* do not emerge into a life of steady victory. The conference at Matlock is specially arranged with a view to helping such believers, not only by giving a sequence of teaching on the basic truths of victory over sin and Satan on the ground of the finished work of Christ at Calvary and the imparted power of the Holy Spirit, but also that believers needing spiritual help may meet with workers able to counsel them and lead them into victory.
>
> In view of the conference, we think it well to reiterate some statements we have from time

> to time expressed in *The Overcomer*, viz: that we are deeply convinced that it is not our commission from God to initiate or lead a "movement" in connection with *The Overcomer* and its distinctive message. We have for many years deprecated the harmful tendency among God's children either to form or join "movements" which, under the idea of advance, tend to separate the members of the body of Christ the one from the other, at a time when unity, on the basis of the finished work of Christ and the sharing of one life between all who are joined to Him, is most essential in the face of a united foe. . . . We are deeply convinced that the great need of today is the building up of the body of Christ. Our aim in *The Overcomer* is this simple ministry of the Word, giving the measure of light we have upon aspects of truth we have learned through deep suffering, and proved as yet in small measure, but sufficiently to know that they are of God for His people. We are aware that they do not meet the need of all believers, but there are those to whom they have come in delivering power and who testify that their lives have been lifted to another plane.
>
> The conference at Matlock will be on simple lines of opening up truth which all the children of God need for aggressive service at the present time; and for the leading of those in bondage into a life of victory.

The keynote of the conferences was informality; no program was planned beforehand. Mrs. Penn-Lewis herself gave the main messages, but the real objective was to be able to spend time in genuine conference and prayer so that those attending had time and opportunity for seeking help concerning the problems they faced and for direct dealing with God. Whitsuntide—the week following Pentecost Sunday—was when these Matlock Conferences were held, and there was a total of three of them: 1912, 1913, and 1914. The "Great War," which began the following August, brought the series to a close.

Those were busy years. It is no light task to edit a monthly magazine and write articles for it. Much more labor was involved than was called for by the original simple book room which her ministry through literature necessitated, especially since all the work was accommodated in her own private home. Because she was so heavily committed, a number of invitations for ministry abroad had to be refused from such countries as Australia, Palestine, America and Germany, among others; but a considerable amount of platform work was still undertaken nearer home. Then in August 1913 she did accept an invitation to spend a few weeks in Finland, which was intended in the main as a holiday but turned out to be something of a working one.

Twelve months later—in August 1914—the First World War broke out. The carnage among the youth of the countries engaged was colossal, and afterwards the whole face of Europe was changed. At the end of 1914 the issuing of *The Overcomer* ceased. Mrs. Penn-Lewis' comment on the six years of publication is illuminating.

> When the paper was commenced six year ago . . . everything was humanly against it. No ordinary steps were taken to announce its advent, for no publisher would have taken the risk of its issue. In fact, when the simple handbill announcing it appeared, a publisher of repute wrote as a personal friend to the Editor in deep concern, anticipating nothing but failure for the paper from a financial and circulatory standpoint.
>
> Therefore, as we look back upon its history, we clearly see that nothing but the hand of God, carrying through a definite purpose ordained by Him, could have upheld and steered the paper; and only the Holy Spirit of God could have guided it to the sorely tried children of God scattered all over the world, and used it to minister to deep needs unknown to all but Him. . . . It penetrated in an extraordinary way to some of the remotest places on the inhabited earth, reaching isolated believers in land after land, to whom it came as a message sent by God, lifting up the crushed and, in some cases, almost wrecked workers, on the eve of being driven from the battlefield.* . . .

> The danger of going beyond the measure of the Spirit in a given piece of spiritual service, because it has become prosperous, is a real one to those who seek to co-work with the Spirit of God. The knowledge of this danger has been of great value in guarding *The Overcomer* from becoming diverted from its ministry. . . . Offers of large sums of money as "capital" to develop it as a journal meeting a deep spiritual need have been made by some who saw its potential, while others of repute have offered to organize prayer circles in connection with it. But from these, as well as from many other propositions, we have, by the grace of God, turned away. We have no commission from God to found or to conduct a magazine developed and worked on ordinary lines, or to build up an organized "work," or to institute a "school of teaching," but only to minister the truth of God to the spiritual people of God, and to remain simply witnesses to the end.

The War years, in spite of the national suffering and anxiety, which she keenly shared, brought a measure of respite for Mrs. Penn-Lewis. After spending the first winter of freedom from editorial work in the Channel Islands, she returned to Leicester in May 1915, hoping to pick up some of her desk work; but almost at once symptoms

---

*This promise was fulfilled in Jessie Penn-Lewis, and the ends of the earth are still being refreshed as a result.

of her old lung trouble recurred. The doctor told her that the magazine had been closed down "only just in time," urged the need of spending the winter away from the cold and damp of England, and spoke very seriously of the care she would need to take in the future.

The monthly conferences (begun in 1909) were carried on in London, Mrs. Penn-Lewis taking part as or when she was able, but often having to pass the responsibility for ministry on to others. In January 1917 it was possible to send out 6,000 copies of an "occasional paper." The replies that came back showed clearly that if, or when, it became possible to resuscitate *The Overcomer*, it would be certain of a big welcome. During this same year Mrs. Penn-Lewis was able to pay two visits to South Wales, which were a tonic to her and signally blessed to many who attended the meetings. Then (while its editor was absent for a period of mission work in South Africa) she edited the quarterly magazine *The Friend of Israel and The Time of the End*—the organ of the Prayer Union for Israel. This gave her an outlet for her written ministry.

There also continued to be a steady outflow of her books and booklets to missionaries and workers in other lands, a special permit having been granted by the government for their dispatch—this being wartime. The following extract from a letter from Persia gives a glimpse of the use fullness of this ministry.

> If my witness as a missionary in a Moslem land is worth anything, I can testify that I count my great spiritual victories over the spiritual hosts of wickedness, both in heavenly and in earthly places, from the day when I learned quite simply, and aloud, to deny ground in my ransomed body and soul and spirit to the devil and his agents; to reassert my freedom from the power of sin on the ground of Romans 6:11; and to reaffirm my trust and confidence in the "law of the Spirit of life in Christ Jesus" according to Romans 8:2. All this I did, sometimes in the operating theatre as I stood giving anaesthetics in the insufferable heat for five hours; sometimes busy in storerooms with madly irritated nerves demanding an outlet; and often in walking about the great hospital compound in the blazing sun; or just before presenting the gospel in my halting Persian to a hall full of dispensary patients. And I am not the only one who has profited by the message of *The Overcomer* in Persia.

The War at last being over, there came a time of readjustment to the new conditions of life. What have since been termed "the winds of change" were much in evidence; work that had been hindered, if not completely stopped by the exigencies of war, had to be restarted under very different circumstances. So it was that in January 1920 *The Overcomer* was again sent out. It was now wisely decided to make it a quarterly, not a monthly magazine; and the policy adopted for its maintenance is still used today. No subscription was charged, but it was sent freely and supplied for by gifts from those moved to send by the Spirit of God. The cost was amply covered quarter by quarter, even when the circulation rose rapidly, and always will be until the Lord shows that its ministry is finished.

The three months that followed the issuance of this first number of the New Series were crowded with evidences of real spiritual fruit. The editor in the second number wrote:

> I must confess that I had not fully apprehended how deep and wide spread was the response to the testimony given in the six years publication of *The Overcomer*. It seems as if we have resumed our paper-fellowship just where we left off at the end of 1914! This is a proof of the work having been of God. No work of human origin would have survived all the testings of these last years.

A Christian worker in California wrote: "It was with almost a sob of relief that I welcomed the first copies of The Overcomer—it was as if reinforcements had arrived to aid in the battle against sin and error."

The same year (1920) saw the revival of her "consultative" conferences, no longer now held at Matlock but at the Conference Center at Swanwick, also in Derbyshire. This first conference showed once more that the special anointing for ministry of the Word rested on Mrs. Penn-Lewis, just as before. Her messages were singularly lucid, and in response to a number of requests they were published in book form under the title *The Centrality of the Cross*—a book which has been of value to many Christian workers over the years and is still exercising a most useful ministry. The following description of one of the meetings gives a sidelight on the atmosphere that prevailed.

> One meeting of this remarkable conference especially lives in the memories of many who were present, when the message of John 12:24 was the theme: "*Except a corn of wheat fall into the ground and die, it abideth alone; but if it die, it bringeth forth much fruit.*" With burning intensity Mrs. Penn-Lewis poured out the message of God which lay at the roots of her own ministry, passionately desirous that others might catch the vision. As the moments sped by, the hearers seemed to lose sight of the speaker and place, hearing only the voice of the Spirit of God calling to a higher plane of life and service than any yet dreamed of as possible. . . .
>
> When the voice of the messenger ceased, a long silence fell upon the gathering, until at last an aged clergyman rose, and in a hushed voice laid before the Lord the longing of the hearts before Him, to be made willing for this pathway of the cross, for "life-out-of-death" fruitfulness in His service through a life tinctured with the very life of God in the human vessel.

Year after year, until her homecall in 1927, these four-day conferences continued; typical attendance was around 250, and one-fifth of these would be ministers. Smaller local conferences were also started in a number of the big cities up and down Britain. They were essentially *her* conferences. At some there were other speakers but she was the mainstay of them. They were now the platform from which the ministry entrusted to her by God was exercised. Now "The Overcomer Testimony," as it was then called, began to take shape.

Mrs. Penn-Lewis herself was always against the formation of a movement; and she might well have agreed with Bishop Ryle's suggestion that "Whitefield was possibly a greater man than Wesley because he founded nothing." On one occasion when she was asked about the future of the work, her reply was: "It will live on in the hearts of those in whom the Spirit has been free to make the cross a reality." One of her favorite pictures of her vision for the spread of the message of the cross was that of the living waters of Ezekiel flowing out from beneath the door of the Sanctuary and in quiet power carrying life and healing far and wide.

It is quite impossible, however, to stop the growth of a movement once it has been launched. It becomes something that tends to take a central position in our outlook and demands to be kept going at all costs. Not only did the number of conferences, meetings, and prayer groups snowball, but "prayer bonds" were formed for ministers, ministers' wives, evangelists, and so on. All this meant more office work and organization, for which workers had to be found. And, of course, there was the Overcomer Book Room and its widespread ministry.

The problem of the future leadership of the work ultimately began to present itself. Mrs. Penn-Lewis was always sensitive about the fact that she was a woman, and wrote articles in defense of the ministry of women. In her case, this was quite unnecessary; God had given her an equipment for the ministry of the Word that could not be gainsaid. But what of later leadership? Most of her closest associates were naturally women, and not all of them were as wise and balanced as she was herself. In fact, speaking confidentially of one of them, she once said, "I hope it will never be possible for _____ to give up working; she will have too much time on her hands, and will go off after some unbalanced teaching."

There were, of course, a number of men who gathered round "The Testimony"; yet her rather wayward ability to judge character sometimes made for difficulties. Differences of outlook and in the interpretation of Scripture began to create division in the ranks, and cliques that were mutually antagonistic began to show themselves. Most of this she had to face and carry alone. But it seems that in His understanding love, the Lord was quietly taking her at her word and leading her deeper into death so that life might be liberated for others. She had so often spoken of the cross as a "crucible"; and now He was gently caring for her in the darkness of trial. The maturity and graciousness of which others were conscious in their dealings with her were ample evidence of His shaping of a vessel that was yielded to Him.

In the midst of these "labors more abundant" the dark cloud of an acute personal trial was creeping up over the horizon the gradually failing health of Mr. Penn Lewis. His work for the city of Leicester during the war years had been strenuous and exacting. By his skillful handling of the finances of the city he had saved its citizens many thousands of pounds, but the long-continued strain and responsibility told heavily upon him. Three months of entire rest, ordered by his physician in 1921, gave only temporary relief, and in the year 1924 it became necessary to resign from his position as City Treasurer and retire, in the hope that his life might thereby be prolonged. And so Mr. and Mrs. Penn-Lewis sold their house in Leicester and moved to a new home in the Surrey hills some sixteen miles south of London.

But the hope that a more genial climate and release from professional responsibilities would effect a restoration of health for her beloved husband was not justified, and on March 24,

1925, William Penn Lewis died. He was laid to rest on the 27th in the Friends Burial Ground in Reigate, Surrey, with a simple, touching service led by Dr. F.B. Meyer. Dr. Meyer remarked that this quiet garden attached to the Friends Meeting House was peculiarly appropriate as the last resting place of William Penn-Lewis, as he was a descendant of William Penn, the founder of Pennsylvania.

The short years until her own homecall in 1927 were struggle all the way. Her health was on the decline. She was working unremittingly. She had to bear bereavement, bringing a weight of loneliness with it. But she faced it all with buoyant courage. How good God was to her! Again and again He poured blessing through her into the lives of others; and again and again she proved the glorious fact that "the eternal God is thy refuge, and underneath are the everlasting arms" (Deut. 33:27). We seem to come back full circle to the verse quoted in the Foreword: "He that believeth into Me, out of the depths of his life shall pour torrents of living water. This spake He of the Spirit."

CHAPTER 8

THE WOMAN HERSELF

I HAVE never forgotten how, when I was very young in the faith, an elderly Christian lady with whom I had been talking suddenly turned and said to me: "My dear, never become super-spiritual!" At the time I was flabbergasted and did not know what she meant. I think that now I am beginning to understand. God loves us all and deals with us as men and women, however long we have trodden the way of the cross. Whatever experiences we have been permitted to enjoy, we never become anything else. You and I are not just "a soul to be saved," we are human beings "subject to like passions" as other folk are. God does not suppress our personality. His life is manifested in *us* and seen through *us*.

Yet it is impossible in a record of a person's spiritual pilgrimage of this kind to avoid obscuring, in some measure, the human side. This final chapter is an effort to convey a just impression of Jessie Penn-Lewis, the woman. She was always thoughtful of others. On one occasion she had invited a very young speaker to give the first message at one of her conferences; she herself was to be the second speaker. Her young partner on the platform glanced at his watch and realized that he had only two or three minutes left of his allotted time. How was he going to round things off? He felt a tug at his sleeve, and Mrs. Penn-Lewis' voice said: "Ten minutes more." Before half that time had elapsed there came a second tug, accompanied by the words: "Go right on." When he had finished, she simply got up, led the meeting in prayer, and closed. On another occasion she launched a young worker into a number of meetings. But when he himself realized that he was not really ready for such responsibility and went and told her, she could not have been kinder or more understanding.

In spite of her unquestioned wisdom in spiritual things, she was not always a good judge of character. On one occasion a girl was introduced to her who was "in service" at one of the large houses not very far from Eccleston Hall, where the Overcomer Conferences were then held and where Mrs. Penn-Lewis had an apartment. The girl produced "a testimony" to a marvelous "spiritual experience," telling of her conversion through the witness of tradesmen who called at the house, as well as a number of others. Mrs. Penn Lewis was impressed, and had her speak once or twice at meetings she arranged for her. The girl turned out to be a fraud!

She had a real sense of humor—a distinct asset to anyone engaged in Christian work. On one occasion one of the minor halls at Eccleston Hall had been rented to an outside body for an evening meeting. No instrument was being used to guide the singing, which that night was particularly mournful and off key. One of her helpers, coming quickly in by a side door, found her sitting on the stairs almost helpless with silent mirth, and was beckoned to sit with her and share her amusement.

She had no patience with false ideas of "separation." Once her host and hostess, during a series of meetings, had insisted on her going to bed early after a strenuous day and were a little surprised to get a message asking if by any chance they had in the house any boys' adventure books, as she wanted something to relax with! On the other hand, she could both speak and write trenchantly about dress or behavior she felt to be unseemly. Fads which *are* sometimes to be found among evangelical believers—about food, medicine, and such like—were also something she took a stand against. A natural simplicity characterized her own life and habits, which was refreshing to see.

Mention has already been made several times in these pages of the continual ill health she carried all through life. One day toward the end of her life a conference was being held in Eccleston

Hall at which she was to speak. About half an hour or so before the morning meeting, one of the office helpers had occasion to go to her study. After knocking on the door and getting no reply, the helper gently opened the door, and there was Mrs. Penn-Lewis bowed over her desk, her head on her hands, apparently in a state of collapse. There seemed to be only one thing to do, and that was to slip into the room, kneel down, and begin to pray aloud. Gradually Mrs. Penn-Lewis sat up, and soon began to pray herself. Then she went straight from the study on to the platform. She led the meetings throughout the day and spoke with such strength and vigor that she could be plainly heard all over the large hall. This was real trust in God and an evidence of genuine courage.

Just occasionally she could go what seemed a bit too far in her claim to have the guidance of the Spirit. One morning she appeared on the platform wearing a new hat, which was a truly astonishing spectacle. Two people who knew her well were sitting together in the meeting. They both sat up in amazement. During her message, as she was seeking to explain that it was possible to know the guidance of the Spirit in everyday life, she said in order to illustrate her point: "For instance, last night He showed me how to trim this hat." To say that the gravity of two of her hearers was tried almost beyond the possibility of control is to put it far too lightly. When dealing with the practical side of the Christian life, she could be caustic if she suspected carelessness. Once when she was talking to a group of ladies who had been discussing "healing" and were seeking her opinion, she asked them if they made sure that their houses were kept properly cleaned and saw that dust was swept from under the beds—telling them bluntly that if they failed to take the normal precautions called for by hygiene, they might expect to have illness in their families and could not ask for "healing" to mitigate their own carelessness.

She was a great believer in righteousness in money matters. Each account concerned with her work was kept separately, and these accounts were closely watched. Money given for one purpose was never allowed to be transferred to something else. If money was short in any particular fund and still did not come in after prayer, she took it that this was an item that was not in God's will and quietly closed it down. Her general attitude to the handling of finance in Christian work is best seen in principles which she herself committed to paper.

> I saw that the conditions of knowing the will of God were these: no "bias" to any path, however pleasant or apparently "good for the Kingdom"; no double motive, however good, e.g., "policy" for the "good of the Kingdom"; no personal aim, however justifiable, e.g., the electing to take a voyage on the Lord's service, and the good of myself as *part* of the motive! The "voyage"

> might be good for myself and the work's sake, but that must not deflect the compass needle of the soul seeking to know the will of God.
>
> The second characteristic of the path of service I have outlined was that, as God opened the doors, so He provided financially (and otherwise) all that was needed to enter them, and this He did apart from all councils and committees. In apostolic fashion, He moved His own hidden saints to "set forward" on her journeys His messenger in a manner "worthy of God." In land after land, as door after door opened, the supply never failed. Only one condition was necessary on the messenger's part—*to keep free to follow the will of God, and that only.*

Mrs. Penn-Lewis was deeply loyal to her friends and co-workers and had a large capacity for affection. The link that bound her and her husband together in their home life was one full of understanding. Over the years his wise counsel and utter unselfishness in the face of constant separation—and even during their times together, her continual absorption in some aspect of the Lord's work—must have proved a joy and blessing to them both. Mary Tugwell, who had become her right hand in the management of the home, as well as her close friend and co-worker, was always spoken of in later years as "my old Mary." After the loss of her husband and of Mary, she was never quite the same. Her love for her

Lord and her sense of commission kept her going bravely on, but life was very lonely. At the same time, the severe pressure caused by dissensions and difficulties in the work took their toll and her physical strength waned.

The final weeks of her life underline the fact that "the gifts and calling of God are without repentance." The Holy Spirit had taken hold of a frail vessel, revealed to her something of the greatness and loveliness of her crucified, living Lord, and empowered her to bear effective witness to Him. She was now 66 years old. A friend who was with her during the last week of journeying and ministry has left us this picture that shows the Holy Spirit still working with and through her. Fittingly her final journey was to Wales and to the Llandrindod Convention.

> During the whole of that last week of her active life there was a peculiar mellow sweetness.... She seemed to be enjoying herself interiorly. To a comment upon the pace at which she was living, she replied, "Oh, this is life to me!" I believe this was so—a grant of grace from above, that she should have that last week of inward relief and outward joy of filling up the full measure of her ministry.
>
> She was ministering, in one way or another, all the week. . . . Evidently it was all with a keen sense of joy at being able. All her messages were in remarkable lucidity and power. I say power,

> but not referring to physical strength, which on at least two occasions seemed flagging, but to the kind of power which conveys the truth to the hearers.

After these meetings she returned to London spent and ill; and only a few days later—August 15th, 1927—was gently and quietly translated into the immediate presence of the Saviour she had learned to love so well, and had served so faithfully. She "was not, for God took her" (Gen. 5:24). She was buried beside her husband in the little God's acre at Reigate.

If I were to try to sum up Mrs. Penn Lewis—the woman—in a few words, it would be something like this: "A Christian lady, whom The King delighted to honor."

PUBLICATIONS
Fort Washington, PA 19034

This book is published by CLC Publications, an outreach of CLC Ministries International. The purpose of CLC is to make evangelical Christian literature available to all nations so that people may come to faith and maturity in the Lord Jesus Christ. We hope this book has been life changing and has enriched your walk with God through the work of the Holy Spirit. If you would like to know more about CLC, we invite you to visit our website:

www.clcusa.org

To know more about the remarkable story of the founding of CLC International we encourage you to read

LEAP OF FAITH

Norman Grubb

Paperback
Size $5^{1}/_{4}$ x 8, Pages 248
ISBN: 978-0-87508-650-7
ISBN (*e-book*): 978-1-61958-055-8

Books by Jessie Penn-Lewis

All Things New
The Awakening in Wales
The Centrality of the Cross
The Climax of the Risen Life
Communion with God
The Conquest of Canaan
The Cross of Calvary
The Cross: The Touchstone of Faith
Dying to Live
Face to Face
Fruitful Living
Life in the Spirit
Power for Service
Soul and Spirit
Spiritual Warfare
Thy Hidden Ones
War on the Saints (Abridged Edition)
The Warfare with Satan
The Work of the Holy Spirit